T0277040

THIRTY
YEARS
OF
FAILURE

THIRTY YEARS OF FAILURE

UNDERSTANDING CANADIAN CLIMATE POLICY

ROBERT MACNEIL

FERNWOOD PUBLISHING
HALIFAX & WINNIPEG

Editing: Candida Hadley
Cover design: Jess Koroscil
Printed and bound in Canada

Published by Fernwood Publishing
32 Oceanvista Lane, Black Point, Nova Scotia, B0J 1B0
and 748 Broadway Avenue, Winnipeg, Manitoba, R3G 0X3
www.fernwoodpublishing.ca

Fernwood Publishing Company Limited gratefully acknowledges the financial support of the Government of Canada, the Canada Council for the Arts, the Manitoba Department of Culture, Heritage and Tourism under the Manitoba Publishers Marketing Assistance Program and the Province of Manitoba, through the Book Publishing Tax Credit, for our publishing program. We are pleased to work in partnership with the Province of Nova Scotia to develop and promote our creative industries for the benefit of all Nova Scotians.

Library and Archives Canada Cataloguing in Publication

Title: Thirty years of failure : understanding Canadian
climate policy / Robert MacNeil.
Names: MacNeil, Robert, 1984- author.
Description: Includes bibliographical references and index.
Identifiers: Canadiana (print) 20190137428 | Canadiana
(ebook) 20190137509 | ISBN 9781773632223
(softcover) | ISBN 9781773632230 (EPUB) | ISBN 9781773632247 (Kindle)
Subjects: LCSH: Environmental policy—Canada. | LCSH:
Climatic changes—Government policy—Canada.
Classification: LCC GE190.C2 M33 2019 | DDC 363.7/05610971—dc23

CONTENTS

For my dad, the wisest person I've yet known.

ACKNOWLEDGMENTS

I'm hugely indebted to all those who have helped and inspired me in one way or another with this book. In particular, enormous thanks goes to the dedicated activists I have been fortunate enough to have met within the Canadian climate movement over the past several years. Their influence provided lots of much-needed inspiration during the process of putting this book together. A huge thanks to my editor Candida Hadley for her keen eye, brilliant insights, and encouragement throughout the drafting and publication process. Thanks also to Beverley Rach, Curran Faris, and the fantastic team at Fernwood for all their help and support. Most importantly are my family and close friends, whose support over the years is incalculable — Mom, Dad, Kayla, Evan, Vince, Christina, Jeannie, Dave, Clarissa, Leigh, and James. The biggest thanks of all goes to Maddy Beauman, without whose love, support, kindness, friendship, and smile, I'd hardly see the point.

PREFACE

In 2015, I was part of a panel event in Toronto organized by a group of local environmental and climate activists. During the Q&A section of the event, one of the attendees presented me with a question that I was embarrassingly underprepared to answer. Her question was: "As a political science scholar who studies climate change, you must have a pretty good sense of exactly why Canadian climate policy keeps failing. Given that knowledge, what *specifically* would you tell a group of activists and ordinary citizens about what needs to be done to fix the situation, and how we can be most effective in creating the changes we want to see?"

The question caught me pretty off guard. So, I did what most academics do when they get a question they can't answer — I bullshitted. I gave a long-winded response that basically amounted to nothing. When I was done talking, I sheepishly said to her, "I hope that sorta answers your question." She looked at me with an unimpressed expression and said, "Meh, not really, but that's fine."

The exchange was unfortunate because her question was a vitally important one. Particularly in a country as complex as Canada — with so many institutional, political, and economic bottlenecks — the climate problem seems so enormous and vexing that it's hard to even know where to start. It's in this context that most climate activism basically amounts to abstract calls for "action," without knowing exactly where to direct one's attention, or what institutions or economic structures to focus on.

This book is an effort to provide a proper answer to the question posed that evening. It draws on political, economic, and cultural research on climate change to give readers a sophisticated understanding of precisely

1

why Canadian climate policy has been such a disaster over the past thirty years, and explains how this knowledge can be used to create the changes that are desperately required if we are going to have any chance of solving this issue.

Big Bay Point, Ontario
2019

CHAPTER 1

THE RISE & FALL OF CANADA'S CLIMATE LEADERSHIP

"It all started out pretty well..."

As one former staffer from Environment Canada noted to me in an interview, "Despite all the calamity that's happened since, the early history of Canadian climate policy actually started out pretty well as I recall."

It was the late 1980s, and after decades of debate the world's scientific community had arrived at a solid consensus around the dangers of anthropogenic climate change. What was required now was for a handful of countries to claim the mantle of leadership and push for bold international action to begin addressing the problem. Unsurprisingly, Canada was at the front of the pack. Unsurprising because we had seen this many times before over the preceding twenty years. Whether the issue was ozone depletion, species extinction, transnational air pollution, or hazardous wastes, if there was a pressing global environmental crisis, Canada was going to use its status as a revered middle-power nation to help lead the international community to a workable solution.

So, it was not terribly surprising that, in 1988, the Canadian government, led by Brian Mulroney's Progressive Conservatives, volunteered to host one of the first major meetings of the international community on climate change. Colloquially referred to as the Toronto Conference on Climate Change, the Mulroney government not only sought to put climate change on the global policy agenda, but it was also among the first governments in the world to propose a potential solution. The Canadian delegation suggested an international "law of the atmosphere," modeled on the existing Law of the Sea, arguing that climate change required a holistic effort that acknowledged the links between all atmospheric issues, and that all members of the international community should have certain duties and responsibilities for ensuring a stable climate for current and future generations.

While Canada's efforts at the Toronto Conference ultimately failed in the face of US resistance, the Mulroney government nevertheless kept up its rhetorical efforts, pledging to fully stabilize Canada's greenhouse gas (GHG) emissions within a decade, and becoming one of the first countries in the world to ratify the United Nations Framework Convention on Climate Change (UNFCCC). Not to be rhetorically outdone, upon forming government in 1993, Jean Chrétien's Liberal government vowed to enhance Canada's efforts on climate change, proposing even stronger targets, along with a series of policy ideas aimed at achieving them.

Indeed, it all started out pretty well.

But, since then…

But Canada's performance since then has been dreadful. Not only did Canada fail to stabilize or reduce its emissions as promised, but its general behaviour on climate has, according to numerous NGOs and partner states, been deplorable. Beginning in the early 1990s, Canada joined a much-maligned coalition of "blocking states" in the UN climate negotiations that consistently sought to weaken and derail any substantive efforts to build a functional global climate treaty. After succeeding in watering down the regulatory framework for the regime, Canada signed the resulting Kyoto Protocol, but failed to take any significant domestic efforts to meet its commitments. In an attempt to create some semblance of action, the Chrétien government implemented a series of weak and ineffective voluntary programs and subsidies for various sectors — which, unsurprisingly, yielded few positive outcomes. As a result, not only did Canada's GHG emissions fail to decline by 6 percent (as formally promised at Kyoto), but between 1990 and 2006, they actually increased by 27 percent, making Canada the treaty's most flagrant violator.

The election of Stephen Harper's Conservatives in 2006 introduced a new level of dysfunction to the situation. After cancelling the Liberals' ineffective climate programs in 2006 (then reinstating them in response to pressure from the electorate in 2007, then watering them down in 2009 to a set of tokenistic window-dressings), Harper proceeded to take Canada's international reputation on climate to a new low. Whether it was muzzling federal scientists to prevent them from disseminating their climate research, ramping up Canadian efforts to disrupt progress at UNFCCC conferences, overturning decades' worth of federal environmental legislation in an effort to provide the oil and gas industry with a more favourable regulatory environment, listing environmental groups as "national security threats" on the Canadian Security Intelligence Service's terror watch list, or allocating millions of extra dollars to the Canada Revenue Agency to run enhanced audits of environmental charities, the Harper government seemed determined to make Canada the world's pre-eminent climate villain. As its biggest act of defiance, however, in an effort to avoid incurring the financial penalties resulting from its abysmal failure to meet its Kyoto commitments, the Harper government formally withdrew Canada from the Kyoto Protocol in December 2011, making Canada the only country in the world to withdraw from the treaty after having ratified it.

In light of Canada's many failures (both domestic and international), the 2016 Climate Change Performance Index issued by the Climate Action Network ranked Canada 59 out of 61 peer countries on climate policy. Canada has also been a perennial winner of the Climate Action Network's "Fossil Awards" for both its non-existent national climate strategy, as well as the Canadian delegation's consistent efforts to disrupt and derail any meaningful progress at international climate negotiations.

In short, Ottawa's behaviour on this matter has, according to Broadhead (2011), moved Canada from a vanguard of multilateralism and environmental protection, to an environmental pariah, and something of a "rogue state." As she contends,

> The concept of a "rogue state" is commonly used to describe states that are either outside international norms and treaties, or in them but presumed to be cheating. Any state that actively blocks, stalls, or otherwise subverts an international process designed in the interests of all becomes a threat to others by virtue of the destructive environmental consequences that are a result of such intransigence.

Indeed, even judging Canada's climate performance in the most charitable terms, it would be difficult to argue that it has not behaved a little like a rogue state.

WHY A BOOK ABOUT CANADIAN CLIMATE POLICY?

The point of this book is not to righteously condemn Canada or Canadians. Indeed, one of the main goals is to duly acknowledge that, relative to many of its peer countries, climate policy in Canada is actually a pretty heavy lift and is beset by a dizzying array of structural complications. As a result, the country's failures over the past quarter century cannot simply be reduced to the agency of a few fainthearted or reactionary leaders (even if, as we will see, such leaders haven't exactly helped the situation). Yet, while these structural factors have made climate action difficult, they nevertheless have much to tell us about what reforms would need to occur in order to resolve the situation. The objective of this book is thus to uncover the main economic, cultural, and institutional factors that have caused Canadian climate policy to continually fail, and thereby draw conclusions about how activists can help incite the radical emissions reductions that are necessary if we are to avoid climate chaos.

Solving this puzzle is important for several key reasons. First, as a G7 country with significant influence in global affairs, Canada helps set the tone for global negotiations and regimes. In the past, Canada has been a major lynchpin in such regimes, helping to bridge divides between major powers on issues of war and peace, trade, human rights, and global environmental governance. In the context of climate change, however, Canada's influence has been toxic. It has set an example for developing countries and peer states that suggests a highly revered nation like Canada can shirk its responsibilities to the global community and future generations and simply get away with it. Understanding and resolving the structural factors that have pushed Canada in this direction is thus key not only for improving Canadian climate policy, but also for restoring Canada's broader position as a force for progress in the world.

Second, Canada is easily one of the worst per-capita carbon polluters on the planet. At 20 tonnes of CO_2e per person, Canada has few equals in terms of greenhouse gas emitters anywhere in the world — indeed, aside from Australia and a handful of small oil-states in the Middle East,

Canada is basically as bad as it gets. When Canada's fossil fuel exports are factored in, it is among the highest net carbon emitters in the world as well. However, as a wealthy democratic society with great capacity for technological innovation and social progress, Canada can begin to restructure its economy in ways that will not only create a foundation for its own prosperity in the twenty-first century, but also set an example for others about how to carry out the types of economic and cultural changes required to address global warming.

Finally, with the election of the Trudeau government in 2015, Ottawa has embarked upon its greatest effort to date to develop a serious national climate strategy. Yet, at the time of writing, we are seeing signs that the approach being put forth is not only extremely weak and unambitious, but rests on an exceptionally fragile political foundation that could crumble at the slightest nudge. The prospect of yet another failure has left activists and concerned citizens enormously frustrated, and has, yet again, confused and dismayed the international community. In this context, it is more important than ever to develop a nuanced understanding of why this keeps happening. One of the central premises of this book is that these failures have all been predictable and avoidable, and that, with an informed and holistic understanding of the situation, Canadians can finally begin to advocate for policies that are both effective *and* politically plausible.

HOW TO READ THIS BOOK

This book is admittedly trying to do two rather different things — both of which are key if we want to have any hope of a safe and stable climate in the coming decades. On the one hand, it aims to provide a simple and pragmatic guide for understanding how activists can create as much change as possible starting *right now*. That is to say, within the institutional, economic, and cultural environment that currently exists in Canadian society, the book tries to explain how ordinary citizens can begin to better navigate the structural minefields that have laid waste to so many climate policy efforts over the past generation (and perhaps even leverage certain tendencies within them) to begin bringing down carbon emissions as quickly and efficiently as possible. To this end, following a brief history of Canadian climate policy, Chapters 3 through 5 try to give a sense of how Canada's dominant structures have produced and maintained such outlandishly high carbon emissions over the years, and how activists can get to work changing this.

On the other hand, the book aims to give a sense of the broader long-term changes that will be required if we want to not merely avoid climate chaos, but also achieve a safe and sustainable form of economy and society moving forward. This task is taken up in the final chapter of the book, which tries to give a sense of what an honest and effective set of climate policies would look like for Canada, and reflects on the bigger structural challenges moving forward around neoliberalism and capitalism itself. It is hoped that this combination of pragmatic, near-term action and philosophical, long-term reflection will equip readers with a good sense of what needs to be done going forward.

CHAPTER 2

A BRIEF HISTORY OF CANADIAN CLIMATE POLICY

The goal of this chapter is not to provide a comprehensive history of Canadian climate policy — this would be well beyond the scope of one brief chapter. Rather, the aim is to simply lay out the gist of the story with an eye toward answering two basic questions. First, what has Canadian climate policy looked like over the past quarter century? And second, how did it come to look this way? The hope is that answering these questions will provide some context for the analysis in the following chapters, and allow us to understand why Canadian climate policy has been such a failure and where the opportunities for progressive change may lie.

This brief history is told in chronological fashion, using the five prime ministerships that governed between 1988 and 2018 as an ordering principle for the story. As we will see throughout the book, however, while the changing federal governments provide a helpful point of reference for telling the story, there is much more to Canadian climate policy than who the prime minister was at any given time. It is, to be sure, a story that takes place across all levels of government and civil society.

THE MULRONEY YEARS: 1988–1993

While debates about the science of climate change had been ongoing since at least the late 1800s, it wasn't until the early 1980s that serious discussions about potential policy responses from governments began to occur. In the Canadian context, the story of climate policy thus begins in earnest at the end of the Mulroney Progressive Conservatives' (PC) first mandate in 1988.

Though it may seem difficult to believe today, the Progressive

Conservative government of Brian Mulroney was actually quite well suited for taking up the task of climate action. At that time, environmental protection had yet to become the thorny, ideological wedge issue that we unfortunately know it as today. Buttressed by the impressive power of the emergent global environmental movement, environmentalism enjoyed broad cross-partisan support in Canada throughout the 1960s, 70s, and 80s. And, for his part, Mulroney was generally keen to make environmental issues a main focus for his government.

To that end, Mulroney appointed influential caucus members to the position of Environment Minister, including Lucien Bouchard and Jean Charest (giving them prominent roles on the Prime Minister's Priorities and Planning Committee — the entity tasked with setting the governing agenda for the cabinet) and began racking up an impressive list of green bona fides. Included among these accomplishments were the Canadian Environmental Assessment Act (which required Ottawa to conduct ecological assessments on any proposed development occurring under federal jurisdiction); the Canadian Environmental Protection Act (which imposed rigorous assessment and management practices around chemical substances); major marine programs aimed at cleaning up the Great Lakes, St. Lawrence River, Fraser River, and Atlantic coast; and the creation of nearly a dozen protected national parks.

But Mulroney's most commendable ecological accomplishments arguably came at the international level, where he positioned Canada as a moral authority behind the global effort to save the ozone layer at the Montréal Conference in 1988, persuaded US President George H.W. Bush to sign the Acid Rain Accord aimed at reducing toxic sulfur dioxide emissions, made Canada the first industrialized country to ratify the UN Convention on Biological Diversity, and helped to secure the appointment of Canadian diplomat Maurice Strong as the Secretary General of the Rio Earth Summit in 1992. In short, in light of Mulroney's efforts, the late 1980s and early 1990s arguably represent the apex of Canada's global leadership on the environment, and for these achievements, Mulroney was, perhaps quite rightly, voted the "greenest" prime minister in Canadian history by *The Magazine for Clean Capitalism*.

1988–1993: Soaring rhetoric, no meaningful action

In keeping with this apparent commitment to environmental issues, the Mulroney government came out of the gate eager to establish Canada as a pre-eminent global leader on climate. To that end, in 1988, the Canadian government hosted one of the first major international conferences on the issue — formally referred to as the World Conference on the Changing Atmosphere — or, colloquially, the Toronto Conference.

In addition to bringing the world together in Toronto to discuss the problem, the Mulroney government also took a first crack at posing a solution. As noted in the previous chapter, in his opening address to the conference, Mulroney called for an international "law of the atmosphere" equivalent to the Law of the Sea. His idea, in effect, was to take a comprehensive, global approach to the issue, which bound together all major atmospheric issues under a single set of international rules that all states and actors would have to follow. While Mulroney's idea was never afforded serious consideration in subsequent negotiations — largely due to opposition from the US delegation — his efforts helped to establish Canada as an early leader on climate.

This budding leadership role remained on display four years later at the Rio Earth Summit in 1992, where Canada not only pushed hard for the creation of the United Nations Framework Convention on Climate Change (UNFCCC), but also became the first industrialized country to formally ratify it. This commitment was codified two years earlier by the government's Green Plan of 1990, which pledged to stabilize Canadian GHG emissions at 1990 levels by the year 2000. At the insistence of the US delegation, however, all such pledges made by national governments at Rio were completely voluntary and non-binding.

In any case, despite the initial display of international leadership shown by Mulroney — along with hundreds of Canadian scientists, diplomats, bureaucrats, and environmental activists — his government did very little to translate this rhetoric into any real policy action. In a move that would soon become standard operating procedure for Ottawa, Mulroney's Green Plan of 1990 centred on information provision and encouraging voluntary action by corporations and provinces on climate. Absent was any mention of regulation, government investments, or any serious strategy to achieve Mulroney's stated goals. Perhaps most importantly, it was Mulroney who would first opt to marginalize Environment Canada in the climate policy process, regarding the agency as "too concerned with the environment, rather than pragmatic responses acceptable to the government" (cited in Smith 2008a). As we will see in the following sections, this impulse to privilege economics and political expediency over environmental protection was to become a hallmark of Canadian climate policy over the following decades.

THE CHRÉTIEN/MARTIN YEARS: 1993–2006

Modern conventional wisdom would tend to suggest that, as power is handed from a Conservative to a Liberal government in Canada, environmental governance is likely to improve. Or, if nothing else, it probably won't get worse. This, however, was not the case when Jean Chrétien's Liberals took over after winning their first of three majority mandates in October of 1993. During the first half-dozen years of Chrétien's tenure as prime minister, Canada's once-proud reputation as a global environmental leader entered into steady decline, as ecological issues were placed squarely on the backburner.

In an effort to tame increasingly problematic federal deficits and debt, Chrétien slashed spending across numerous federal agencies — Environment Canada not least of which — thus significantly wounding their regulatory capacities. In this context, Chrétien balked on initial efforts to enact or strengthen nearly a dozen pieces of crucial environmental legislation, including the Endangered Species Protection Act, the revised Fisheries Act, the Species at Risk Act, legislation implementing the UN Convention on the Law of the Sea, and the Drinking Water Materials Safety Act. More importantly, however, in an effort to both reduce federal spending and provide a greater sense of autonomy to the provinces, Chrétien began a process of transferring federal authority on the environment to the provinces. On several issues, this led to a watering-down of national standards and enforcement, as certain provinces capitalized on the opportunity to provide a pared-back regulatory regime for polluting industries. The result was that, by 2001, the International Development Research Centre ranked Canada 93 out of 180 countries on environmental protection, and 28 out of 29 industrialized countries on ecological governance (D. Boyd 2002).

Nevertheless, during his last couple years as PM (2001–2003), Chrétien unexpectedly went to great lengths to improve his government's environmental record. Commentators have never reached a firm consensus on why this sudden change of heart occurred. Perhaps Chrétien was tired of the scorn he was receiving from NGOs and partner states on Canada's declining environmental performance. Perhaps he sensed it was his final opportunity to build a progressive legacy for which he could be remembered fondly. Or perhaps Chrétien had always had deep sympathies for the cause of environmentalism and finally had an opportunity to act without economic constraints (Canada's budget was firmly in the black by his third mandate) or political considerations (Chrétien seemed to acknowledge that the party would not let him contest another election as PM after the 2000 campaign). Whatever the reason, in his final two years Chrétien oversaw the passage of several major environmental laws (including the Species at Risk Act, Pest Control Products Act, and National Marine Conservation Areas Act), announced the creation of ten new national parks, and began to restore Environment Canada's capacity by injecting billions of dollars of new funding into the agency.

1993–1995: Modest effort, no substantive action

The Liberals' 1993 election campaign gave no indication that the coming years would bring such a marked decline in Canadian environmental leadership. In fact, the party's platform promised one of the strongest ecological performances in Canadian history, including a pledge to surpass Mulroney's climate policy ambitions by reducing national GHG emissions to 20 percent below 1990 levels within a decade (Macdonald 2008).

To deliver on this pledge, Chrétien created a multi-stakeholder negotiation process under the guise of the National Action Plan on Climate Change (NAPCC). The process brought together federal and provincial energy and environment ministers — along with representatives from major industrial sectors and other affected parties — to try to generate a consensus on the most effective ways to reduce national emissions (Smith and Macdonald 2000).

Early on in the process, the opposing sides of the debate made their positions clear. Environmental groups claimed they would settle for nothing short of coercive regulatory mechanisms capable of forcing compliance from big polluters. On the other side, representatives of emissions-intensive industries (led by oil and gas), along with the governments of fossil-fuel rich provinces (led by Ralph Klein's PC government in Alberta) made clear that they would not stand for any policy interventions that raised energy prices or operating costs. For these latter groups, the only options worthy of consideration were so-called voluntary mechanisms that would allow industry to act of its own accord. In particular, they made it clear that the imposition of a federal carbon tax would be taken as a declaration of war against them. Seeking to de-escalate the tension, Chrétien declared to an audience in Calgary that a carbon price was never going to be on his agenda: "Relax, relax...," he calmly assured the crowd. "It's not on the table, and it will never be on the table" (cited in Macdonald 2008).

In addition to the turmoil within the stakeholder consultations, there was also a deep rift from the start within the federal cabinet and bureaucracies. On the one side, Environment Canada (headed by Environment Minister Sheila Copps) advocated decisive action on climate and argued for strong regulatory mechanisms to do so. On the other, Natural Resources Canada (headed by Anne McLellan — who was, incidentally, Chrétien's Alberta Lieutenant, and one of only four Liberal MPs elected from the province) sought to protect the interests of resource-rich provinces and extractive industry. McLellan thus advocated the voluntary approach favoured by industry and cautioned that interventionist action by Ottawa would effectively exterminate what little remained of the Liberal Party in Alberta.

By early 1995, the alliance consisting of heavy industry, the Alberta government, and Natural Resources Canada was clearly winning the battle. In February 1995, the Chrétien government unveiled an impressively weak national climate strategy called the Voluntary Challenge and Registry Program (VCR). Standing as the centrepiece of Ottawa's climate policy, VCR asked all major industrial emitters to publicly register their voluntary plans to reduce carbon emissions, and proposed some potential strategies that industry could choose to adopt if they saw fit.

1995–1997: From hero to villain & back:
Canada & early UNFCCC negotiations
This domestic dysfunction would soon be reflected in Canada's declining international leadership on climate. As UNFCCC signatory states began negotiations around how to structure a global climate regime, it became

clear early on that the EU, along with most of the developing world, was going to push hard for a governance system based around ambitious and binding emissions targets for rich/high-polluting countries like Canada. The rationale for rich countries taking the lead was relatively straightforward. Under the principle of "Common but Differentiated Responsibilities," the wealthy, industrialized countries that had emitted the lion's share of existing carbon into the atmosphere would begin developing cleaner technologies and experimenting with climate policy options during the treaty's first commitment period. As these countries began to work the new technologies down the cost curve and sort out the most effective forms of climate policy, developing countries would likewise commit to substantive action during subsequent commitment periods, and begin adopting cleaner technologies in turn.

For Chrétien, this focus on countries like Canada was bad news. It was not lost on him that his government's VCR program was far too weak to generate any emissions reductions, and that the tumult of the NAPCC process and the fierce opposition of several provinces was going to make any such efforts very difficult. Indeed, with no meaningful or systematic way to reduce emissions, even the modest voluntary target Mulroney had pledged at Rio appeared completely implausible. Caught between the impulse to maintain Canada's tradition of environmental leadership and the reality of the domestic climate policy process, what was Chrétien to do?

For reasons that will be discussed at length in the following chapters, Ottawa responded by aligning with an emergent grouping of states referred to as the "JUSCANZ coalition" — an acronym for its initial founding members: Japan, the US, Canada, Australia, and New Zealand. Early on in the UNFCCC process, JUSCANZ made it clear that its primary objective was to prevent a climate regime based on binding targets and timetables (Harrison and Sundstrom 2007). Additionally, they expressed strong opposition to any regime that would excuse developing countries from the need to cut their emissions during the first commitment period — thus belying the notion of a historical burden of responsibility for industrialized countries. And finally, JUSCANZ demanded that the regime include a series of so-called flexibility mechanisms — emissions trading and offset markets — which critics viewed as loopholes intended to water down the regime's effectiveness (Smith and Macdonald 2000).

JUSCANZ quickly took on a villainous reputation among much of the international community. At the first Conference of Parties (COP I) in Berlin, JUSCANZ infuriated the environmental community by managing to scrap the global consensus around capping emissions at 1990 levels by 2000. Most offensive to environmentalists, however, was the coalition's implicit connection to the infamous Global Climate Coalition — a lobby organization funded mostly by large oil, coal, and gas companies — which expressly aimed to sow doubt about the scientific consensus around climate change. Early on in the UNFCCC process, the Global Climate Coalition frequently accompanied the US delegation to meetings and exercised a great deal of influence over its position (Broadhead 2011).

In the lead-up to COP 3 in Kyoto, Japan — the conference at which a formal treaty was to be established — Ottawa had to settle on a national emissions target to submit to the UNFCCC. Negotiations among federal and provincial ministers of environment and energy landed on the idea that Canada should stick to the Mulroney government's earlier pledge to simply reduce emissions to 1990 levels, but with the caveat that the timetable should be pushed back a decade to 2010, instead of 2000. With the provinces and major industry more or less on board, Chrétien appeared to have navigated a political minefield relatively well.

Suddenly, however, Chrétien had an unexpected change of heart. Immediately prior to the Kyoto conference, US Vice-President Al Gore signaled that the US would be willing to take on a much more ambitious target than initially expected. In line with this development, President Bill Clinton directly reached out to Chrétien, imploring him to likewise pledge a stronger target in order to help bridge the divide between the EU and JUSCANZ and hopefully arrive at a functional and effective regime (Harrison and Sundstrom 2007).

Accordingly, Chrétien instructed the Canadian delegation to increase its pledge to one percentage point behind the US's pledge. After being told on the conference floor prior to the final alphabetical roll call that the US was committing to a target of 7 percent below 1990 levels by 2012, the delegation called Chrétien to get his blessing for a -6 percent target. With the Prime Minister's consent, Canada formally pledged to reduce national GHG emissions to 6 percent below 1990 levels by 2012.

While green groups and partner states applauded the Canadian delegation's change of heart, provincial leaders and industry representatives were fuming. In making this decision, Chrétien did not consult a single provincial premier or minister, nor had Ottawa ever done an economic analysis of what a 6 percent reduction would mean for the national and provincial economies. Indeed, Chrétien's unilateral retreat from the hard-won federal–provincial agreement destroyed any remaining semblance of trust and cooperation in the delicate national climate policy process.

So why did Chrétien do it? Why did he blow up this fragile consensus for which he had worked so hard? The following chapters will try to give a more articulate sense of why we see these types of cognitive dissonance throughout the history Canadian climate policy. At an ideational level, many would argue that the impulse to maintain Canada's image as a "good global citizen" carried the day, and Chrétien refused to be embarrassed by the Americans massively outpacing the Canadian pledge — even if he knew such a target was unrealistic. At an economic level, one could argue that Chrétien simply bowed to pressure from his country's largest trading partner, acknowledging that Canada risked trade retaliation or border adjustment taxes if it tried to secure such an unfair advantage over the US.

Whatever the case, Chrétien was likely reassured by JUSCANZ's success in securing the aforementioned "flexibility mechanisms" as part of the final deal. Indeed, throughout the negotiations, Ottawa bargained exceptionally hard for these mechanisms, and demanded, in particular, that each tonne of CO_2 absorbed by Canadian forests be allowed to count as a tonne's worth of pollution credits under these programs. In theory, this would allow Canada to increase its GHG emissions by over two billion tonnes per year (or a 12 percent *increase* over its Kyoto target) without falling into non-compliance (Harrison and Sundstrom 2007). For these underhanded efforts, the Climate Action Network awarded Canada the infamous "Fossil Award" at Kyoto — a badge of shame presented to the country that argues for the most regressive policies and ideas.

1998–2001: The calm after the storm

Chrétien's unexpected intervention at Kyoto seemed to foreshadow a new round of intergovernmental warfare between Ottawa and the provinces. But, in fact, the three years immediately following Kyoto stand as one of the more tranquil moments in the history of Canadian climate policy. This is largely because, likely sensing that he had massively overstepped at Kyoto, Chrétien immediately went to the ten premiers with three reassuring promises.

First, Chrétien promised Ottawa would undertake a detailed economic analysis of the Kyoto target before his government proceeded to actually ratify the commitment in Parliament (ratifying a treaty officially codifies the promise in Canadian law, and makes it, in effect, illegal for the government to defy it). Second, he promised that no province or region would ever be asked to shoulder a disproportionate burden of Canada's climate policy efforts. And finally, Chrétien vowed that all future efforts to design a strategy to fulfill Canada's commitment would be undertaken in full partnership with the provincial governments (Harrison and Sundstrom 2007).

For anti-Kyoto provincial governments like that in Alberta, these three promises were very reassuring indeed. They all seemed to indicate that there was still a good chance that ratification might never actually occur. Indeed, Chrétien himself noted in an interview soon after the Kyoto conference that, while he certainly hoped to see the Accord ratified in Parliament, "we have seen some treaties in the past that have not actually been ratified" (cited in Harrison and Sundstrom 2007). Moreover, even if ratification did occur, Chrétien's dual promises that federal climate policy would be designed in full consultation with the provinces and that no region would be forced to bear an unreasonable burden seemed to suggest that provinces like Alberta could either effectively veto the policy, or at least strip it of any regulatory power — just as it had done with the NAPCC process.

As a result of this newfound calm, for roughly three years following the turmoil of the Kyoto process Canadian climate policy basically went dark. With Ottawa remaining very gentle and cautious in the ongoing federal–provincial discussions, there were few signs of any real turbulence or unrest. There were also few signs that any real progress was being made toward a substantive plan to reach Canada's Kyoto commitment. But, at least for the moment, the waters were calm.

2001–2002: The US bails, the provinces revolt

But this calm would not last forever. The next galvanizing incident was to occur in early 2001 when, soon after his inauguration as US president, George W. Bush announced that the US would not ratify Kyoto on his · watch. As National Security Adviser Condoleezza Rice told German Chancellor Gerhard Schröder, the Bush administration considered Kyoto to be "dead" (Borger 2001).

In truth, it was never likely that the US would ratify Kyoto anyway. In the US system, only the Senate can ratify international treaties. And in mid-1997, the Senate unanimously passed the famed Byrd-Hagel Resolution, which banned the US from entering into any climate treaties in which large developing countries like China and India were not required to accept similar targets to the US. Nevertheless, Bush's explicit declaration brought an end to the polite fiction that the US was still a part of the treaty and forced the world to re-evaluate its future. This was particularly the case for Canada, given that its Kyoto pledge was, by many accounts, a political chess move designed to keep pace with its southern neighbour. But with Washington now removed from the equation, a chorus of critics from the provinces and industry demanded that Canada leave as well.

But Chrétien refused. Why he chose to do so is undoubtedly a complex matter (and, indeed, the following chapters will look in depth at some of the political and economic factors that influenced his decision), but, if nothing else, Chrétien probably sensed an interesting opportunity in the US's withdrawal. As it happened, in order for Kyoto to officially take effect under international law it had to be ratified by states contributing at least 55 percent of rich-country emissions (or, in the language of the treaty, 55 percent of "Annex 1" state emissions). With the US now out of the equation, there was no room for error. Pretty much every other industrialized country would have to ratify if Kyoto was to have any chance of surviving — most importantly Japan, Russia, and Canada. In this context, the EU suddenly became much more accommodating toward the remaining JUSCANZ members, and the Canadian delegation in particular became increasingly audacious about its demands.

Specifically, the delegation demanded that Canada be allowed to count "carbon sinks" (e.g., maintaining and enhancing the carbon storage capacity of Canadian forests) as part of their national effort, and receive more generous credits for facilitative forestry and land management practices. While these same demands had been staunchly rejected at previous COPs, they were grudgingly granted at COP 7 in Bonn following the US withdrawal. In total, Canada would receive a credit for 30MT (or nearly one-sixth of its Kyoto commitment) for land and forestry practices already underway (e.g., business as usual measures).

For Chrétien, this appeared to be a tremendous diplomatic victory that would provide great credibility in his negotiations with the provinces. But, to his dismay, most provinces could hardly have cared less about this win. And when Chrétien soon gave indications that his government would unilaterally move toward ratification in light of the success in Bonn, the stage was set for a new round of intergovernmental warfare.

2002: The battle over ratification

Chrétien's announcement in the autumn of 2002 that Ottawa would move forward with ratification was, by any metric, an extraordinarily brazen thing to do, and would launch the most heated and contentious battle in the history of Canadian environmental politics. The Prime Minister's declaration fully coalesced a powerful anti-Kyoto alliance led by the province of Alberta, the oil and gas lobby, the Alliance Party, the Progressive Conservatives, an influential group of business associations (including the Canadian Council of Chief Executives, the Canadian Federation of Independent Business, the Canadian Manufacturers and Exporters, and the Canadian Chamber of Commerce, among others), and the province of Ontario (where Premiere Mike Harris claimed he wouldn't support ratification if it killed even one single job) (Smith 2008b). In addition, Chrétien had to contend not only with major divisions within the federal bureaucracy and multiple ministries, but also within his own caucus and cabinet, where dozens of Liberal MPs made their opposition clear. Indeed, by the time the ratification debate reached the floor of the House of Commons, Chrétien only had the stated support of two provinces — Québec and Manitoba — neither of which was prepared to dedicate even a fraction of the time, energy, and resources to the cause as the anti-Kyoto coalition.

As the debate heated up, several actors within the anti-Kyoto camp formed an umbrella group called the Coalition for Responsible Energy Solutions. Along with the government of Alberta, the group spent millions of dollars on ads across the country focused on making several arguments to the public. Included among these were the ideas that Kyoto would cost the Canadian economy hundreds of thousands of jobs; result in $40 billion per year in lost GDP growth; create higher taxes, higher prices, and higher costs of living; require Canada to redistribute its wealth to rapidly growing countries that refused to accept GHG targets; and render Canadian businesses uncompetitive with American companies (Smith 2008a). They claimed, moreover, that Canadian contributions to global warming were tiny by international standards, and that ratifying Kyoto would create enormous economic pain for miniscule environmental benefit (Macdonald 2008).

While the pro-Kyoto coalition (led by the Chrétien government and a handful of green groups) had nowhere near the ubiquity or passion of their opponents, it nevertheless tried valiantly to defuse the attacks and make a case in favour of ratification. Their argument rested on three pillars. First was an economic argument, which claimed that the attacks against Kyoto amounted to little more than shameless fear mongering, and that ratification would, in fact, create new wealth by providing Canadian companies access to rapidly growing green markets worth billions of dollars. Second was a security argument, which focused on the extent of Canada's vulnerability to the physical and geopolitical effects of a warming world. But most prominent was a moral argument, which drew on the notion of Canada as "good global citizen," always willing to do the right thing, and not afraid to show leadership in the face of American inaction (Smith 2008a).

Despite the withering attacks from the opposition, Chrétien announced his intention to hold the parliamentary vote over ratification in early December of 2002. Though he knew that, if necessary, the NDP and Bloc Québécois could be counted on to provide the votes required to pass the measure, Chrétien was wary of the potential for embarrassment if dozens of Liberal MPs made good on their vows to oppose the government. To avoid this, the Prime Minister took the unusually extreme measure of declaring the resolution a matter of confidence (parliamentary resolutions are almost exclusively considered to be "free votes" in the Canadian system) and promising that he would refuse to sign the nomination papers of any caucus member that voted against the government (Harrison and Sundstrom 2007).

With this impressive show of force, on December 10, 2002, a resolution calling upon the federal government to ratify the Kyoto Protocol easily passed the House with a vote of 195 to 77. It did so with the unanimous support of the Bloc Québécois, NDP, and Liberals — though fourteen Liberals were absent — and unanimous opposition of the Alliance and PC parties. Three days later, the formal decision to ratify was made by the Cabinet, and on December 17, 2002, the Government of Canada filed its ratification papers with the United Nations.

2002–2003: Nothing happens

The Chrétien government's ratification of Kyoto is arguably one of the braver and bolder acts of federal policy in modern history. Indeed, as we saw, it marked an instance in which, facing enormous opposition from some pretty powerful political and economic forces, Ottawa strove to do the right thing. Nevertheless, in spite of its valour, the ratification vote changed almost nothing. In a practical sense, all of the political and institutional dysfunction that had plagued Canadian climate policy since the late 1980s had not gone anywhere. While Ottawa was free to ratify whatever climate treaties it wished, all of the policy levers required to actually implement effective climate policies and bring about significant emissions cuts still belonged to the provinces. In short, while the Chrétien government had won the battle over ratification, they surely had not won the war over national climate policy.

The policy strategy tasked with bringing about these emissions cuts and making good on Canada's commitments was released at the end of 2002. Officially titled A Climate Change Plan for Canada, the strategy left much to be desired, and clearly reflected the institutional complexity Ottawa faced. The plan included no provisions for direct regulation, carbon pricing, or any other form of corrective intervention on the part of the federal government. Instead, it proposed a series of so-called negotiated covenants with industry to reduce their emissions, spending programs aimed at supporting technological upgrades, and the purchase of international credits to meet the remainder of Canada's commitments (Government of Canada 2002).

Importantly, however, the plan included very few specifics. In terms of the negotiated covenants, Ottawa provided no details on which sectors would be asked to make cuts. In terms of spending, the plan provided no details on how much money would be allocated, nor to which projects or efforts. And in terms of the plan's various musings about potentially revising building codes and transportation strategies, the government offered no details about how it would compel the provinces to implement these changes on its behalf. Indeed, as Harrison and Sundstrom (2007) succinctly suggest, more than decade after Canada made its first formal pledge to cut emissions, and after several massive national consultation exercises aimed at achieving those cuts, the Chrétien government "effectively released a plan to develop a plan."

In any case, with Chrétien's tenure as prime minister coming to a close in 2003, the difficult task of designing a real plan to fulfill Canada's Kyoto pledge (now in the face of skyrocketing national emissions) would fall to his successor, Paul Martin.

2004–2005: New leader, same results

By the time Paul Martin took over as Liberal leader and prime minister in December 2003, it was still somewhat unclear how he intended to proceed on climate policy. Since at least the late-1990s, Martin had been jockeying to take over the party's leadership following Chrétien's eventual retirement. To this end, he carefully avoided taking strong positions on many policy issues that were seen as divisive within the caucus and party. On climate change, in particular, Martin tended to speak only in generalities about his views, speaking vaguely about the need for action, but never delving into specifics.

Upon taking office, however, Martin gave indications that he favoured decisive action, and wanted to see Canada return to a position of global leadership on the issue. The rhetorical height of this ambition came in 2005 when Canada hosted COP 12 in Montréal. Commenting on the Bush administration's decision to abandon Kyoto, Martin suggested that the US lacked a global conscience and invited President Bush to visit the Canadian arctic so he could witness firsthand its rapid warming. While Martin's comments willfully overlooked the fact that the US's emissions performance was far better than Canada's, the anti-American rhetoric seemed to slightly rehabilitate Canada's image within the UNFCCC.

In an effort to finally produce a substantive strategy to reduce emissions, Martin decided in 2005 to scrap the Chrétien government's plan for negotiated covenants and establish a national cap-and-trade scheme using the regulatory authority afforded to the federal government under the Canadian Environmental Protection Act. Under the Act, Ottawa has the power to regulate any "toxic" substances in the environment, with a toxin defined as anything that may have an "immediate or long-term harmful effect on the environment" or which may create a "danger to the environment on which life depends" (Government of Canada 2017). In light of this rather ambiguous definition of toxins, GHGs were deemed to fit within the Act's mandate. Nevertheless, many regulated industries resented the notion of having their products or activities defined as toxic, given the obviously negative connotation of the term. In response, Martin sought to appease critics by deleting the term "toxic" from the Canadian Environmental Protection Act's wording, and replacing it with the term "harmful" — thus allowing Ottawa to regulate GHGs because they were harmful, not toxic.

Martin chose to package this revision together with his government's 2005 budget bill, anticipating that the opposition Conservatives would never be so foolish as to bring down his minority government over a tiny semantic change to an obscure passage in an old statute — particularly given that the opposition was in no shape to fight an election and had spent hours consulting on the budget. But Martin was wrong. Conservative leader Stephen Harper decried the move as a backdoor effort to impose a carbon tax on Canadian families, and vowed to vote against the budget bill, thus bringing down the government and forcing an election. Martin promptly retracted the amendment, and backed away from the idea of a cap-and-trade system (Harrison and Sundstrom 2007).

As an alternative, in its final year, the Martin government proposed a climate strategy called Project Green. In keeping with the approaches of the Mulroney and Chrétien governments, the plan avoided any talk of carbon prices or regulation and focused instead on providing industry with federal subsidies to hopefully inspire voluntary emissions cuts. As with the strategies of his predecessors, Martin's plan was woefully inadequate, particularly given Canada's skyrocketing emissions as the Alberta oil sands underwent unprecedented expansion.

In January 2006, the Martin government lost its bid for re-election, thus bringing an end to the Liberal Party's thirteen-year effort to act on climate change. Though Chrétien and Martin both spent a fair bit of political capital in their efforts to move forward on the issue, history will record that they both failed. While both individuals undoubtedly had good intentions, this would prove to be no match for the overwhelming political, economic, and institutional challenges that have come to characterize Canadian climate politics and policy. While the Liberals managed to ratify a stronger than anticipated emissions target under Kyoto, they nevertheless ran headlong into enormous opposition from the provinces and industry, and were hamstrung by division within the federal ministries and bureaucracies, as well as the Liberal caucus and cabinet. Under such conditions, it became nearly impossible to develop an effective national climate strategy. In an effort to save face, the years spanning 1993–2006 saw the development of several inadequate plans aimed at trying to coax industry into making modest emissions cuts with fistfuls of taxpayer money. As a result, by 2006, not only had Canada's emissions not declined by the promised 6 percent below 1990 levels, they had increased by roughly 27 percent, inviting shame and condemnation from much of the international community.

THE HARPER YEARS, 2006–2015

Try as one might, it is difficult to find anything particularly positive to say about the Harper government's environmental record. Put simply, by almost any metric, Harper would easily be considered the most anti-environmental prime minister in modern history. Over the course of his decade in office, Harper effectively laid waste to Mulroney's notion that a Conservative government could be a vigilant guardian of the nation's ecological heritage, and, in so doing, helped to redefine environmentalism as a caustic wedge issue between conservatives and progressives.

While Harper's two minority governments (2006–2008 and 2008–2011) maintained a relatively centrist orientation (carefully scripting positions on issues like the environment in a prudent effort to allay perceptions that the party was "too right-wing" to be trusted with anything but a minority government) the real story began with the attainment of a majority government in 2011. It was at this point that the Harper government grew increasingly radical on the environment, undertaking an unprecedented and unabashed assault on the federal government's system of ecological protections. Instead of tabling several hundred smaller bills, Harper quietly packaged all of his environmental rollbacks into a single omnibus budget implementation bill officially titled the Jobs, Growth and Long-Term Prosperity Act. Passed in May 2012, the bill dedicated more than two hundred pages of text to rolling back the broad scope of federal environmental governance, including sweeping regressive changes to the federal Environmental Assessment Act, Species at Risk Act, Fisheries Act, National Energy Board Act, Navigable Waters Protection Act, and the complete elimination of the country's National Roundtable on the Environment and Economy, and Kyoto Implementation Act. The intended effect of these rollbacks was to optimize the operating space for extractive industries by reducing protections of the country's air and water quality, abolishing decades-old protections for wildlife and their habitats, radically reducing the scope for public participation in environmental assessments, and neutralizing the power of the assessment process by moving it away from independent panels and into the hands of the Prime Minister's Office.

Perhaps most disturbing, the Harper government took up a bizarre campaign to delegitimize Canadian environmental groups by consistently depicting them as "radical," "foreign funded" "extremist groups" that sought to harm Canadian resource development (cited in MacNeil 2014a). In 2012, Harper added a section on these groups to the government's anti-terror strategy, noting that it had to be vigilant in monitoring and responding to extremism that is "based on grievances — real or perceived — revolving around the promotion of various causes such as animal rights, white supremacy, and environmentalism" (ibid.).

2006–2008: Harper reneges, provinces step up

If there is anything positive one could say about Harper's new approach to climate policy beginning in early 2006, it's that he was at least slightly more honest about the situation than his predecessors. While Chrétien and Martin continued to keep up the positive rhetoric despite the dismal results, Harper, upon taking office, simply declared that it was now effectively impossible for Canada to reach its Kyoto target, and gave every indication that his government had no desire to even try. This lack of interest in climate policy did not come as a surprise to most observers. As leader of the Canadian Alliance in 2002, Harper's views on climate change first made national news when, in a speech to his caucus, he suggested that Kyoto was nothing more than a "socialist scheme to suck money out of wealth-producing nations" based on "tentative and contradictory scientific evidence."

Keeping with these views, just a handful of weeks after taking office, Harper began gutting the climate programs his predecessors had put in place — even the exceptionally modest voluntary ones that were at least giving the illusion of federal action. As part of the rollbacks, he scrapped Martin's Project Green, along with the industry subsidies that were supposed to produce 80 percent of the program's emissions reductions, and canceled several billion dollars' worth of federal spending to promote energy efficiency and green technologies. Perhaps most importantly, however, Harper sent a clear message to the provinces that, after nearly a decade and a half of acrimonious negotiations, the federal government would no longer be hassling anyone to make deals on climate policy. Indeed, for all intents and purposes, Ottawa was, until further notice, out of the climate policy business.

This change of leadership and attitude in Ottawa would soon make itself felt on the international stage as well. While one might have anticipated an immediate Canadian withdrawal from Kyoto, Harper was eager to avoid the domestic and international fallout from such a bold move, particularly as he only maintained a minority government and was keen to build a stronger base in Québec (where Kyoto remained very popular). In this context, Harper decided that Canada would remain formally involved in the UNFCCC talks, but only for the purpose of trying to bend the process to his will. Beginning at COP 12 in 2006, the Canadian delegation made clear that it had once again returned to its early/mid 1990s position that formal targets and timelines must be off the table, and that all actions by states should be voluntary. Much like the old days, Canada was once again being accused of sabotaging the talks, with one report describing Canada as the "black hatted villains" of the UNFCCC process (cited in Smith 2008a). Indeed, gone was the rhetorical Liberal language of Canada as the good international citizen and environmental leader. For NGOs and partner states in the climate process, Canada was increasingly a pariah state.

Unfortunately for Harper, however, his plan to quietly push climate policy to the backburner was dramatically interrupted in early 2007. Seemingly out of nowhere, climate change surged in national polling to stand as the issue about which a plurality of Canadians cared the most. Indeed, a January 2007 poll showed 26 percent of respondents citing the environment as the single most important issue on their mind, overtaking traditional top-tier issues like the economy and healthcare. As *The Globe and Mail* noted, environmental issues have suddenly "developed a top-of-mind salience the likes of which we've never seen before ... In 30 years of tracking, we've never had over 20 per cent saying this is the most important issue" (cited in Macdonald 2008).

This came as unwelcome news for Harper, who, eyeing a majority government in the next election, knew he had to appear responsive. To that end, less than a year after gutting Martin's Project Green, Harper more or less reinstated the program. Repackaged under a new plan entitled Turning the Corner, the government announced $4.5 billion in new environmental spending, consisting mostly of tax incentives for businesses, subsidies for home and building retrofits, and support for climate initiatives at the provincial level. As part of the announcement, the government declared that it was committed to reducing national emissions by 150 MT by 2020. While this sounded like a good step on first inspection, it intentionally overlooked the fact that Canada's Kyoto target required a reduction of 300 MT by 2012. The announcement was, thus, a formal rejection of Canada's Kyoto commitment.

Climate change's sudden surge in opinion polling had another major consequence — one that will become a major part of the story going forward. In 2007, bowing to the growing public support for climate action (and acknowledging that the federal government was not going to take the lead), several provinces began to take up the issue themselves. British Columbia got the ball rolling when, under the leadership of Premier Gordon Campbell, the government set a target of reducing provincial emissions to 33 percent below 2007 levels by 2020, and implemented North America's first revenue-neutral carbon tax to achieve that goal. Later that year, Ontario, Manitoba, Québec, and British Columbia all joined several US states in forming the Western Climate Initiative to discuss the formation of a cap-and-trade system for carbon emissions. Finally, in an effort to deflect attention away from the increasingly grim global reputation of its oil industry, Alberta developed its own climate strategy, with the goal of reducing carbon emissions 14 percent below 2005 levels by 2050 (which is really just a polite way of saying 18 percent above 1990 levels).

2008–2011: Dion's gamble; Washington re-engages

The years of 2008 and 2009 would prove to be two of the most consequential in the unfolding drama of Canadian climate politics. After a seemingly endless period of inaction, both Canada and its biggest trading partner — the US — would undergo bruising national election campaigns in which climate change featured prominently.

Although polls indicated a gradual decline in the public's attention to environmental issues throughout early 2008, Liberal leader Stéphane Dion decided to make a revenue-neutral carbon tax a key plank in his party's platform for the subsequent election. Released in June 2008, Dion's Green Shift proposed a new tax on fossil fuels starting at $10 per tonne and rising by $10 each year until 2012. This was to be offset by a series of tax cuts elsewhere that would, in theory, make the Green Shift revenue neutral for Ottawa and create no new net costs for Canadians.

While Dion's plan enjoyed lukewarm support even under ordinary conditions, two additional factors helped to desecrate it further. First was the relentless attacks from all points on the political spectrum throughout the 2008 election campaign. On the left, the NDP used the occasion to depict themselves as populist champions of the working class, claiming that the Liberals' plan would place onerous burdens on struggling Canadian families. The NDP thus countered with a cap-and-trade program focused solely on large corporate polluters — overlooking the fact that higher operating costs for industry tend to be passed on to consumers, as well as the offsetting tax cuts in the Liberal plan. But far more resonant were the attacks from Harper's Conservatives, who sought to turn the election into a referendum on "Dion's new tax on everything." With a ferocity and pervasiveness rarely seen in Canadian electoral campaigns, the Conservatives inundated the public with messages on radio, TV, internet, t-shirts, and even gas pump screens about the Liberals' "insane" tax that would "screw Canadians," especially young families, seniors, and rural Canadians (MacNeil 2016).

This approach was aided by a second key development — the onset of a major global economic downturn in the middle of the campaign. Indeed, the spectre of a global financial crisis allowed the Conservatives to fully overwhelm what little support remained for the Green shift, framing it as an extremely risky economic experiment that could plunge the country into perhaps the deepest recession in its history and even threaten national unity (Harrison 2012a). Just to make sure there was no confusion about the choice facing voters, the Conservatives promised a series of new tax cuts for Canadian families, including a significant tax cut on diesel.

While the election of October 2008 was never solely a referendum on Dion's carbon tax, it proved to be a tremendous burden for the Liberals, as most of the campaign was spent trying helplessly to defend the imposition of a new tax in the middle of a recession. And the results were plain to see. The Liberals had one of their worst showings since Confederation, losing a quarter of their seats in Parliament, and receiving their lowest ever share of the popular vote. Soon after the election, Dion conceded the tax was a mistake and stepped down as leader. His replacement, Michael Ignatieff, likewise acknowledged that the Green Shift was poorly conceived and indicated that he had no plans to pursue a similar program.

For approximately three weeks following the October 2008 election, Harper's position on climate policy seemed to have been vindicated. All indications suggested that the electorate had largely backed away from its momentary focus on environmental issues, and indeed the Conservatives had been re-elected with even more seats — albeit still short of Harper's coveted majority. Underscoring his government's strengthened position on the issue, Harper authoritatively declared in the House of Commons that his government "will not — and let me be clear on this — aggravate an already weakening economy in the name of environmental progress" (cited in Taylor and Barrett 2009).

But the election of President Obama less than a month later appeared to dramatically reshape the field. Obama had made climate change a fairly prominent aspect of his campaign platform, and, immediately upon taking office in January 2009, instructed his Democratic majorities in the House and Senate to begin crafting an economy-wide cap-and-trade program for him to sign into law. Obama's ambitions on climate policy created unwelcome pressure on the Harper government for a couple key reasons. First, it effectively undermined Harper's argument that Canadian action on climate would undermine competitiveness with the US. But second, and more importantly, Democrats in Congress had included two key measures in their legislative proposals that could potentially have devastated many Canadian businesses. The first was a "border adjustment tax," where financial penalties would be levied on imports from countries that did not have similar carbon regulations in place. And second was a "low carbon fuel standard," which would have discouraged US refineries from buying Alberta's oil, given the higher emissions created by oil sands refinement (Harrison 2012a). In light of these threats, Harper acknowledged the need to move forward with a national cap-and-trade program, as well as a stronger federal fuel economy standard.

But, given the US's own dysfunctional climate policy process, Obama's cap-and-trade program was killed by his own party in Congressional negotiations less than nine months after his inauguration. Acknowledging the impossibility of a legislative solution, Obama turned to his executive authority and instructed his Environmental Protection Agency to begin the process of regulating GHG emissions under the federal Clean Air Act.

Following suit, Harper soon announced that his government had no intention of moving forward on cap-and-trade, and that he intended, at some point in the future, to develop a sector-by-sector regulatory approach, harmonized with the US strategy.

2011–2015: Requiem for a national climate policy
While Harper's inaction on climate during his first two minority governments was a constant source of indignation for environmentalists, few could have anticipated how grim the situation would become after his majority victory in May 2011. No longer encumbered by a minority parliament or permanent election campaign, Harper was more or less free to enact his agenda as he wished. And he wasted little time.

Immediately following their victory, the Harper government began working on plans to significantly reduce federal oversight of extractive industry in an effort to accelerate energy and resource development, particularly the Alberta oil sands. This objective took on heightened importance after the Obama administration announced it would delay a decision to approve expansion of the Keystone XL oil pipeline — a 1897 km pipeline that would have carried more than 830,000 barrels of oil each day from Alberta down to refineries on the US gulf coast.

Foreshadowing the reforms to come, in December of 2011, Environment Minister Peter Kent announced Canada's formal withdrawal from Kyoto, calling the treaty an "impediment" to progress on climate change, while also noting that Canada's only hope of meeting its Kyoto target at this point would require "removing every car, truck, ATV, tractor, ambulance, police car and vehicle of every kind from Canadian roads, or closing down the entire farming and agriculture sector and cutting heat to every home, office, hospital, factory and building in Canada" (cited in Walsh 2011).

The government's March 2012 budget gave a further sense of Harper's intent. The budget slashed Environment Canada's funding by nearly 10 percent, leading to the elimination of close to one thousand full time positions (MacNeil 2014), and took aim at dozens of agencies engaged in environmental science research — including the Canadian Foundation for Climate and Atmospheric Research, which was forced to close after its funding completely dried up. In total, the budget slashed more than $3 billion in spending and approximately five thousand jobs from science-based departments responsible for monitoring the country's air, water, atmosphere, and wildlife — a move which the Professional Institute of the Public Service of Canada suggested could only be described as a "political purge" (PIPSC 2011). The budget further shut down the Polar Atmospheric Research Laboratory (a vital climate science observatory station in the Arctic), canceled the National Round Table on the Environment and the Economy, and provided $8 million in additional funding for the Canada Revenue Agency to launch aggressive audits of environmental groups across Canada.

As noted in Chapter 1, the apogee of this effort came the following month in April 2012, when the government passed its omnibus budget implementation bill. Clocking in at over four hundred pages, the Jobs, Growth and Long-Term Prosperity Act stands as the largest environmental bill in Canadian history — one that did not enhance a single environmental protection.

By far the most consequential rollback was a complete overwriting of the Canadian Environmental Assessment Act — a law that imposed rigorous environmental assessments on all resource development projects across the country. The newly passed version of the Act removed all requirements for environmental assessments on projects deemed minor, as well as major projects that are proposed, endorsed, or regulated by the federal government — thus allowing the Prime Minister's Office (PMO) to completely control when and where the Act is enforced. In this context, the bill scrapped more than three thousand outstanding assessments, many of which were in the oil and gas sector. Under the new Act, if a pipeline project were selected for federal assessment it would no longer be referred to an independent or arm's-length panel, but rather assessed in-house by the PMO.

The new Act also limited public participation in assessment hearings to individuals who are "directly affected" by the project or are deemed to have "expertise" on the issue (though these qualifiers are not defined). Additionally, the Environment Minister was provided with new powers under the Act to pre-emptively disband any independent panel and move the assessment back in-house if it appears it will not be completed on time. Finally, when an assessment identifies significant negative impacts from a proposed project, the new Act allows the Environment Minister to transfer decision-making powers back to the Cabinet, where it can make the final decision on whether a project can proceed in spite of its environmental impacts.

The bill also removed all time limitations on project permits that affect species at risk and/or their habitat (permits which were previously set at three and five years, respectively, and ensured reviews to evaluate ongoing impacts on species at risk), and completely exempted pipeline applications from their requirement to include impacts on species at risk and their habitats. Finally, the bill changed the Coasting and Trade Act to allow greater offshore drilling on all of Canada's coasts, including a newly announced 9050 km^2 of Arctic waters that was to be open for bidding, and eliminated reporting requirements for greenhouse gas emissions.

During the latter three years of Harper's majority mandate, the government skillfully avoided any real action on climate with the use of stall and delay tactics. This mostly consisted of a perpetual promise that Ottawa would soon begin regulating industry on a sectoral basis, and that details of such regulations would be released at some point in the near future. Part of this was a long-stated promise to regulate emissions from the oil and gas sector — the details for which the public had been forced to wait over seven years. However, in December 2014, with crashing world oil prices, Harper withdrew this pledge, telling the House of Commons that doing so would be a "crazy" idea. Indeed, by the time of the federal election in 2015, the government had successfully passed nearly a decade without ever putting any of these long-promised sectoral regulations in place.

As noted above, there are few positive things to say about Canadian climate policy under Harper. If the Mulroney, Chrétien, and Martin governments were a tale of a rhetorically committed federal government running into the enormous political dysfunction of Canadian climate policy, the Harper government was a more naked and honest expression of that dysfunction. For most observers, Harper's government simply did not care about climate change and wasn't ashamed to let it show. For many Canadians, the worst element of this was the international embarrassment and ridicule Harper's government invited upon the country. After 2006, Canada's influence and prestige within the UNFCCC — and perhaps the international community more generally — underwent a marked decline, as many governments and NGOs came to view Canada as a villainous spoiler. The United Nations Development Program went so far as to single out Canada's climate position in its 2008 annual report, deeming it a threat to the world's collective future (Chaloux 2015).

Perhaps most disappointing was the fact that, by the end of the government's tenure, all of this destructive posture seemed to be for not. With the dramatic crash of world oil prices in mid-2014 — and Canada's subsequent prolonged flirtation with recession — Harper's promise of Canada as an emergent energy superpower seemed to be dead on arrival. Estimates suggested that the sharp decline in oil prices caused more than 100,000 job losses across the country, as a raft of multinational firms rapidly abandoned the oil sands for fear of losing billions of dollars in stranded assets (MacNeil and Paterson 2016).

If the Harper era can be said to have a silver lining, however, it is undoubtedly the spate of provincial climate policies that took root between 2007 and 2015. Disillusioned with the lack of action from Ottawa (and facing their own internal pressures to act), British Columbia, Québec, Ontario, Manitoba, and even Alberta all stepped up and implemented their own programs. In British Columbia, the Liberal Party's carbon tax successfully endured its first several years, managing to survive multiple election cycles without a significant backlash. In 2013, Québec introduced a cap-and-trade scheme for the industrial and electrical sectors that was linked with California's trading system. In Ontario and Manitoba, pledges were made by the ruling governments to implement cap-and-trade systems similar to Québec, and likewise link them with California's. And finally, with the shock election of the NDP in Alberta's 2015 election, not only was the province's Specified Gas Emitters regulation maintained, but a new and more ambitious set of policies was developed (see Chapter 3).

THE TRUDEAU YEARS: 2015–2019

After nearly a decade of Conservative rule in Ottawa, the October 2015 federal election saw Justin Trudeau's Liberals shock the country by skyrocketing from 34 to 184 seats to secure a robust majority government. For environmentalists across Canada and the world, Trudeau's victory was met with a combination of joy and caution. On the one hand, the gloomy Harper years were over and Canada finally appeared to have a federal government willing to play a constructive role in global and domestic climate governance. But at the same time, this was the same

Liberal party that made countless unmet promises on climate for over a decade, all while overseeing a dramatic expansion of national carbon emissions. Perhaps Trudeau, for all his good intentions, would be hamstrung by the same conditions that laid waste to the climate goals of Mulroney, Chrétien, and Martin.

Nevertheless, the change of approach from Harper was impossible to miss. Trudeau immediately created a cabinet committee on climate change, and had the Canadian delegation take on several prominent roles at COP 21 in Paris, including serving as a key contact group coordinating negotiations between states — a position that would have been unimaginable during the Harper years. Moreover, Canada announced several other new policies at Paris, including a major increase in funding for the UN's Green Climate Fund for developing nations, the elimination of federal subsidies for fossil fuel, and support for lowering the UNFCCC temperature stabilization target from 2°C down to 1.5°C (MacNeil and Paterson 2016).

At the domestic level, Trudeau quickly set to work negotiating the details of a national climate strategy. While he declined to discuss the specifics of his plan on the campaign trail, Trudeau was clear on two key things. First, he would *not* increase Ottawa's emissions target beyond Harper's pledge of 30 percent below 2005 levels by 2030. And second, he would let the provinces take the lead on developing a national climate strategy, limiting Ottawa's role to merely facilitating an overarching nationwide framework.

When the Trudeau government set to work on the deal in late 2015, there had arguably never been a more optimal time to negotiate such a deal. In terms of public support, opinion polls conducted in January 2016 indicated that nearly 60 percent of Canadians favoured a national price on carbon and wanted the federal government to take the lead on the issue (McCarthy 2017). But more importantly, for the first time in modern history, none of Canada's largest provinces had a Conservative government in power. Unlike the failed intergovernmental climate negotiations of the 1990s and early 2000s, Trudeau would find himself sitting across the negotiating table from pro-climate majority governments representing Ontario, Québec, BC, and (most importantly) Alberta. In fact, with the lone exceptions of Manitoba, Saskatchewan, and Alberta, the Liberal Party was in power in every province from coast to coast. Additionally, both major federal opposition parties were in no position to put up a fight, as both the Conservatives and NDP would spend most of Trudeau's first two years engaged in protracted leadership battles after their respective electoral drubbings in 2015.

In addition to having a general sympathy for Trudeau's climate objectives, most provincial governments also saw a tremendous opportunity to extract various ransoms from the federal government in exchange for their support. The main request was for greater healthcare transfers, which had been pared back during the Harper years. But by far the most significant request came from Alberta NDP Premier Rachel Notley, who made support conditional on Ottawa green-lighting construction of the proposed Kinder Morgan Trans Mountain Pipeline expansion, which would twin with an existing pipeline and thereby allow Alberta to ship 890,000 barrels of oil each day to BC's coast, increasing tanker traffic in Burrard Inlet more than seven-fold. Despite his reticence toward the pipeline during the 2015 campaign, Trudeau approved the request and offered the BC Liberal government a sweetener in the form of a $1.5 billion Ocean Protection Plan to enhance the environmental integrity of the BC coast.

In one of the more remarkable feats of intergovernmental cooperation in recent history, in December 2016, the premiers of eight provinces and three territories signed on to the deal, formally titled the Pan-Canadian Framework on Clean Growth and Climate Change. The accord set new regulations on heavy industry, increased fuel efficiency standards, invested in clean energy innovation, and earmarked federal funds for installing renewables and decommissioning coal-fired power plants. At the centre of the deal was an agreement that each province would establish a price on carbon emissions, starting at a minimum of $10 per tonne in 2018, and rising by at least $10 each year to reach a minimum of $50 per tonne by 2022. Under the terms of the agreement, each jurisdiction would be allowed to fulfil this obligation by establishing either a carbon tax or a cap-and-trade system, with all resulting revenue to be kept by the province or territory to spend as they wish. Those that failed to do so would have a carbon tax unilaterally imposed on them by Ottawa (for an explanation of the difference between a carbon tax and cap-and-trade system, see Appendix 1).

Saskatchewan and Manitoba, both governed by conservative governments, were the only provinces that refused to sign the deal. Despite having Canada's largest per-capita carbon emissions, Saskatchewan Premier Brad Wall (an avowed climate sceptic) rejected the treaty, insisting it would impose significant harm on the province's oil, gas, coal, agriculture, and mining industries, and dramatically increase the cost of electricity from its coal-fired power plants. Likewise, Manitoba Premier Brian Pallister refused to sign, arguing that his province should receive credit for its past efforts to shift to hydroelectric power. Both provinces soon indicated their intentions to sue Ottawa, arguing the federal government had no constitutional power to force the provinces to adopt a carbon price.

The Manitoba/Saskatchewan altercation aside, by early 2017, the Trudeau government's climate strategy appeared to be proceeding smoothly. His government had made the political calculation to trade an oil pipeline for a carbon price (for a discussion on the merits of this decision, see Chapter 6) and it seemed to be working out. But this relative progress was abruptly disturbed in May 2017, when BC voters went to the polls in what would turn out to be a fateful provincial election. During the campaign, the opposition NDP and Green parties both took tough positions against the Kinder Morgan pipeline and pledged to do everything possible to derail the project if elected. When the election resulted in a hung parliament, the Green Party agreed to a "confidence and supply" deal to allow the NDP to form a government, led by John Horgan as the new Premier. With BC's new Premier promising to prevent construction of the pipeline expansion (thus casting doubt on Alberta's future compliance with the climate accord), Trudeau's carefully choreographed plan for a national climate strategy appeared to be coming unglued.

When Horgan soon delivered on his promise (and backed legal challenges from Indigenous communities and threatened to deny construction permits for the pipeline), the Kinder Morgan Corporation officially abandoned the project. In a last-ditch effort to save the pipeline (and thereby keep Alberta in the climate treaty), the Trudeau government responded by announcing that Ottawa would use federal funds to purchase the existing Trans Mountain Pipeline from the company for a price of $4.5 billion, and invest several billion more to build the expansion pipeline with public money.

But despite Trudeau's best efforts to keep all the provinces willingly in the treaty, the following months would see his goal of a consensus-based national climate strategy fully unravel. By mid-2019, most of the pro-climate premiers who'd signed the deal in 2016 had gradually lost their re-election bids, only to be replaced by considerably more reactionary individuals. This was most pronounced in the two largest emitting provinces, Ontario and Alberta, both of which elected staunchly anti-climate premiers (Doug Ford in Ontario, and Jason Kenney in Alberta), and subsequently scrapped their respective carbon pricing legislation. As a result, by mid-2019, a group of provinces representing more than 75 percent of Canada's emissions (Saskatchewan, Manitoba, Ontario, and Alberta) had become non-compliant with the treaty, threatening to make the whole effort worthless. With its hand forced, the Trudeau government made the bold decision to unilaterally impose a carbon price on these provinces.

At the time of writing, it remains uncertain what the consequence of this action will be, as these provinces remain locked in a tense legal battle with Ottawa over its constitutional ability to make such an imposition. Moreover, it remains highly uncertain whether *any* of Trudeau's climate strategy will remain popular enough to become institutionalized over the coming years, as conservative opposition parties at the federal and provincial levels continue to successfully stoke a populist backlash against them. And, perhaps most importantly, even if these policies are maintained, it remains unclear whether any of these policies will prove remotely capable of making any kind of significant dent in Canada's enormous rate of GHG emissions. What is clear, however, is that thirty years on, Canadian climate policy remains as dysfunctional and uncertain as at any point in its long, frustrating history.

WHAT TO MAKE OF IT ALL

This thirty-year snapshot paints an admittedly gloomy picture. From an environmental perspective, there are, indeed, very few positive takeaways. What is perhaps most noteworthy is the remarkable consistency from one government to the next in terms of an inability to create effective legislation, meet modest targets, craft solid intergovernmental deals, obtain the support of industry, or maintain credibility within the international community. Indeed, despite the supposed enviable green credentials of Mulroney's Progressive Conservatives, or the soaring green rhetoric of the Chrétien/Martin Liberals, or the supposedly more honest approach of the Harper government, or the pragmatic consensus building of Trudeau, Canada has remained one of the world's pre-eminent climate laggards. While Stephen Harper's policies were undeniably jarring for most environmentalists, his approach was actually largely consistent with all of his predecessors: blame the previous government for making unrealistic promises, make new promises with no serious plan to achieve them, promote a dramatic expansion of extractive industries, and oversee an increase of national emissions.

In that context, a key premise of this book is that, when seeking to understand these broad trends in Canadian climate policy, it turns out that individual governments, political parties, and leaders actually seem to matter very little. Indeed, in the time since climate change emerged as a serious policy issue in the late 1980s, Canada has had six different prime ministers, from three different major political parties, presiding over ten different parliaments. And with the exception of some small (but not insignificant) moves at the provincial level and a faint glimmer of hope under Trudeau, there has been thirty years of failure on the issue.

For that reason, this following chapters try to uncover the *structural* factors that have informed and inhibited the approaches of all governments and leaders during this period. In so doing, it is hoped that we can arrive at a deeper understanding of why Canadian climate policy has been such a dismal failure — and uncover opportunities for a more effective approach.

CHAPTER 3

POLITICAL INSTITUTIONS

For better or worse, institutions structure our existence. While we may prefer to think of our lives as the products of freewill and unfettered choice, the truth is that, from the day we are born, our lives are deeply embedded in an array of institutions that not only structure our worlds, but also provide the filters and context for understanding and making sense of them. As Douglas North (1991) famously defined them,

> Institutions are humanly devised constraints that structure economic and social interaction. Throughout history, they have been devised by human beings to create order and reduce uncertainty, and produce a distinctive combination of sanctions and incentives that shape patterns of political influence and organization, and lead political and economic actors toward some kinds of behavior and away from others.

While this formal definition may tend to imply a certain static and/or neutral quality to institutions, in the realm of Canadian climate policy, they are anything but. As we'll see in the following pages, some of these institutions (Canadian federalism and Aboriginal land title) have been evolving in dramatic ways for the better part of 150 years, and the current shape of national climate policy can only be understood as part of this sequential story. Nor are institutions necessarily a set of neutral brokers between competing interests. Rather, as we will see in the section on Canada's first past the post electoral system, institutions can be quite blunt in the way that they structure and predetermine outcomes so as to benefit one set of interests over another. Indeed, as this chapter will highlight, the story of Canadian climate policy is very much a tale of institutions helping to predetermine the outcome.

INSTITUTION #1: CANADIAN FEDERALISM

Under most circumstances, federalism can be an enormously boring topic to study. But in Canada, nothing could be further from the truth. The story of Canadian federalism is, in many ways, the story of Canada itself. Whether binding together as a national family to engage in great acts of nation building, or hurdling toward the brink of disintegration in narrow secession referenda, this institution has been an enduring feature of Canada's story. And climate policy is no exception. Of all the major political and economic institutions that have influenced the shape of Canadian climate politics and policy, it is safe to say that none has proved more consequential than federalism.

In one sense, this is not entirely unusual. While coordination challenges are present in all countries trying to develop a national climate policy, federated systems (where a country is comprised of multiple states or provinces with constitutional authority to make and enforce laws — e.g. Canada, Australia, the US, etc.) have an especially daunting task. In contrast to unitary countries (where the national government has supreme authority — e.g. France, Japan, the UK, etc.), federal systems must balance a wide range of divergent regional interests and cultures, and try to overcome a collective action problem that can sometimes rival the one faced by the global community. In a federated system, attempts to cut carbon emissions in one state or province are effectively moot if others increase theirs by an equal or greater amount. Federal governments must therefore develop sophisticated strategies that reduce the temptation for individual states/provinces to free ride, while at the same time manage to secure significant national reductions. Given that ten of the eighteen biggest carbon polluters (in absolute terms) are federal systems, Canada is not alone in trying to solve this puzzle (D. Gordon 2015a).

But in another sense, Canada is somewhat alone. There is arguably no other federal system in the world with as bizarre a history and constitutional structure as Canada's. Not only has Canadian history been an often painful intergovernmental battle over provincial autonomy that has rendered Ottawa extremely timid to intervene on major issues like climate change, but the Constitution was almost perfectly designed to incite a turf war over this particular issue. As a result, as we'll see below, federalism has proved to be one of the most frustrating and enduring causes of climate policy stagnation over the past three decades.

Federalism & climate policy around the world

By global standards, the climate performance of federated vs. unitary countries is actually quite mixed, suggesting that the mere presence of a federal system is neither necessarily helpful nor prohibitive. According to Christoff and Eckersley (2011), there appear to be two general trends at work in federal systems that can either be beneficial or burdensome.

On the one hand, some federations display a pattern in which experimentation with new forms of climate policy at the state/provincial level lead to growing momentum for nation-wide action. Given the policy lessons the federal government is able to learn from these experiments, some of the most effective and well-designed climate policies in the world have their origins in federal systems. Examples of this pattern can be found in Germany, the European Union, and even the United States, where the failed American Clean Energy and Security Act was largely based around a program developed in a handful of Northeastern states. Moreover, this dynamic tends to be amplified when states/provinces find themselves in a so-called race to the top with one another, where they compete to implement the best climate policies in an effort to attract new green-tech industries and jobs to their jurisdiction.

On the other hand, federal systems can also create enormous roadblocks for climate policy. In particular, there are several instances around the world where concentrations of negatively impacted industries and communities in certain states/provinces have created stubborn "veto coalitions" in the federal legislature. The most prominent example is perhaps the US, where coal mining stands as a major economic activity in at least twenty-six individual states. While these states may have comparatively small populations, they nevertheless control more than half of the federal Senate, and have thereby managed to render formal climate legislation a non-starter.

Whether a federal system will fall into the latter or the former camp generally depends on two key determinants. First is the country's constitutional division of powers. If the state/provincial governments have regulatory jurisdiction over GHG emitting activities (for example, mining, electricity generation, building codes, transportation, etc.), they will typically be in a much stronger position to prevent federal climate policy from taking effect. In such a situation, the important variable is which parties hold power at each level. If both federal and subnational governments are in favour of action, it is more likely to occur. If one or both levels feature governments that are hostile to climate policy, it becomes rather unlikely.

Second is the regional allocation of costs. In general, if the most powerful states/provinces are negatively impacted by climate action, they will have a disproportionate capacity to stop national legislation. Canada is a prominent example of this, where Alberta (acting on behalf of its oil industry) and Ontario (acting on behalf of its manufacturing industry) played a crucial role in preventing federal action throughout the 1990s and early 2000s. On the other hand, if the most powerful states are in favour of action and face relatively low costs from climate policy, they can create powerful momentum for changes at the federal level. The European Union is an example of this, where countries like the UK, France, and Germany put strong pressure on the rest of the union to adopt ambitious climate policies, which were later implemented at the EU level.

Constitutional ambiguity & Canadian climate policy

The biggest single problem as it relates to Canadian federalism and climate policy is the fact that, constitutionally speaking, it is not at all clear which level of government is actually in control. When the Constitution Act of 1867 was drafted and passed into law, environmental issues were not a prominent concern for governments or society generally (indeed, Canadian confederation predates the modern environmental movement by nearly one hundred years). As a result, the document is, in effect, completely silent on which level has legislative or administrative power on environmental matters (Bélanger 2011). As environmental case law has evolved since the 1960s, the question has only become murkier, with the Supreme Court determining that both levels can create and enforce environmental policy when acting on the basis of one of their listed constitutional powers.

For the provinces, the argument for jurisdiction over climate policy is indeed ample. Their constitutional control over all natural resources within their borders means they have authority over oil, gas, and coal mining, as well as any other GHG-intensive extractive industries. Their jurisdiction over publicly-owned Crown land (which constitutes roughly 90 percent of Canada's land mass) means they have control over agricultural policy and most major land development projects within their territory. And their control over municipal institutions and all "local matters" means that they also have constitutional power over things like building codes, electricity generation, transportation planning, etc. (Cameron and Simeon 2002). All of these items are crucial to a strong climate policy, and, indeed, the provinces have sole jurisdiction over all of them.

By contrast, Ottawa's jurisdictional claim over climate policy is slightly more ambiguous, and is rooted in a handful of considerably less direct constitutional clauses. The first is that, according to the Constitution Act of 1867, the federal government has authority over any issue or problem that crosses provincial or international borders (which climate change, as a whole, clearly does). Second, it has jurisdiction over any issue or problem that could potentially have national economic or security implications for Canada (which, climate change clearly will). Third, Ottawa has constitutional control over taxation, trade, and commerce policy (all of which it could arguably use to, for example, implement a carbon tax, or influence the use of resources like coal, oil, and gas). And finally, though not without *enormous* complication, Ottawa could intervene on climate change by citing its constitutional duty to ensure "peace, order and good government" within the federation (Bakvis and Brown 2010).

While the framers of the Constitution may have intended that most of the issues now associated with climate policy be left to the provinces, Ottawa nevertheless does appear to have all the powers needed to unilaterally legislate and administer a national climate policy (Brown 2012; Macdonald 2008). The obvious question then is, why have pro-climate governments in Ottawa refused to do so?

There are a few reasons. First, as Kathryn Harrison (2002) argues, one of the key reasons Ottawa has typically preferred to let the provinces lead on environmental policy is simply to avoid electoral blame in the event that the resulting program is unpopular. As noted in Chapter 2 (and further discussed in Chapter 4), Canadians tend to be rather non-committal when it comes to environmental policy, favouring it when times are good, and shying away from it when times are bad. As Harrison suggests, Ottawa has, in many cases, opted to simply pass the buck on environmental policy, preferring to let the provinces incur any resulting backlash from an angry electorate.

Second, a comprehensive national climate program is bound to be quite expensive, requiring billions of dollars' worth of investment in bureaucratic and technical capacity. And in an era when Ottawa is trying to reduce spending and offload more responsibilities to the provinces, taking on this type of program at the federal level is clearly an unattractive option.

But to really understand why Ottawa has been so loathe to act on its capacity over the past thirty years, one must fully appreciate the enormously complicated and often extremely painful history of Canadian intergovernmental relations over the past 150 years. As we'll see below, the Canadian federation is unique for how incredibly acrimonious it has been over the years, even coming within a small margin of breaking apart on two different occasions. As a result, modern governments in Ottawa are extremely nervous about provoking regional discontent by impinging upon provincial jurisdiction.

Canadian Federalism: A *Very* Brief History

1860s — 1930s: Quiet, peaceful relations
In most respects, the first seventy years of Canadian intergovernmental relations were reasonably peaceful, featuring only a few momentary instances of bitterness. To a large extent, this relative peace stemmed from the fact that, unlike many federations around the world, the Canadian Constitution of 1867 was actually quite clear in detailing which powers were assigned to which level of government and featured very few areas of shared jurisdiction between Ottawa and the provinces. Indeed, under the Constitution, provinces were given sole legislative and administrative jurisdiction over any area considered to be "local" — for example, schools, hospitals, property, municipalities, natural resources, etc. Ottawa, by contrast, was limited to maintaining control over a relatively small handful of "national" concerns — for example, defense, trade, commerce, banking, and currency — as well as the broadly defined task of making laws to ensure the "peace, order and good governance" of the Canadian federation. This narrowly defined division of powers — coupled with the country's relatively small economy, minimal offering of public services, and tiny government bureaucracies — created little space for the two levels to bump heads and ensured that both sides stayed in their own lanes. Indeed, beyond a bitter debate over national conscription during the First World War, intergovernmental relations during this period could be characterized as relatively calm and stable (Cameron and Simeon 2002).

1940s — 1950s: Cooperative federalism & the welfare state

In the two decades immediately following the Second World War, however, the intergovernmental landscape changed dramatically. As national economies across the Western world expanded at breakneck speeds, countries like Canada began building expansive national welfare states to counter the ills of rapid industrialization. For better or worse, this project ushered in a dramatically expanded role for the federal government, given that, while many of the newly developed programs fell squarely within provincial jurisdiction under the Constitution (e.g., healthcare, education, social assistance, etc.), the vast majority of the funding and policy design came from Ottawa. While this enhanced role for the federal government created numerous conflicts and difficulties along the way, on the whole, the federation adapted reasonably well. Over time, close professional relationships were established between federal and provincial officials, leading to a new era of so-called cooperative federalism in Canada (Bakvis and Brown 2010).

1960s — 1970s: Deteriorating relations

But the peace and cooperation of the early post-war era did not last long. By the mid-1960s, Québec's Quiet Revolution was unmasking a powerful progressive nationalism within the province that not only transformed Québec society from top to bottom, but also fundamentally challenged established ideas about Canadian federalism and the Constitution. At the same time, growing regionalism in Western Canada was creating similar concerns and tensions regarding the appropriate role for Ottawa in provincial affairs. This was further compounded by an increasingly assertive attitude in all of the provincial capitals as their budgets, responsibilities, and bureaucracies grew along with their expanding economies, populations, and welfare states.

With this rapid expansion of the public sector at both the federal and provincial levels, Ottawa and the provinces increasingly bumped heads. As their lists of responsibilities and competencies continued to grow, many provinces became less willing to permit federal intervention or defer to Ottawa's leadership, preferring instead to pursue their own ambitions and develop their own mandates. These mounting tensions were exacerbated by the election of Pierre Trudeau's government in 1968. With his belief in the need for a strong central government to develop and oversee a uniform economic and social policy from coast to coast, Trudeau aggravated the growing turf war between the two levels of government. This was particularly the case with regard to Ottawa's relations with Western Canada and Québec — the latter of which elected the separatist Parti Québécois to power in 1976. Indeed, under Trudeau's rule, the era of cooperative federalism largely faded away, replaced by a new mood of mistrust and competition.

Early-1980s: The boiling point

By the early 1980s, the mounting political and ideological battles over the role and nature of Canadian federalism reached a climax. Following the Québec government's failed attempt at winning a referendum that would have granted it a mandate to formally secede from Canada, Trudeau's Liberals moved forward with two key policies that further pushed intergovernmental relations to the brink. On the one hand, Trudeau's efforts to repatriate the Canadian Constitution with or without provincial consent further inflamed Québec's growing nationalism. On the other hand, Trudeau's National Energy Policy — in which Ottawa unilaterally assumed centralized control over the production, sale, and export of energy resources across the country — caused an explosion of resentment and alienation in Western Canada, particularly Alberta. Indeed, at a time when tensions were already high, these two policies brought the temperature to a boiling point, forcing the country to reflect on some extremely difficult questions about the real long-term value of the Canadian federation.

Mid-1980s — early-1990s: Mulroney tries to break the fever

With the election of Brian Mulroney's Progressive Conservatives in 1984, the state of intergovernmental relations changed yet again. Securing one of the biggest majority governments in Canadian history (complete with a plurality of seats in every single province and territory, as well as one of the largest popular vote victories in modern history), Mulroney promised to usher in a new era of intergovernmental peace and goodwill. To that end, upon entering office, the new Prime Minister quickly dismantled the National Energy Program and vowed to engage in close consultation with every province on important policy decisions. Among Mulroney's more impressive acts of intergovernmental coordination was the signing of the

Meech Lake Accord in 1987 — a treaty designed to persuade Québec to endorse the Trudeau government's constitutional amendments of 1982 by providing greater decentralization of powers in certain areas and formally recognizing Québec as a distinct society.

In spite of his best efforts, however, Mulroney was unable to put an end to the intergovernmental acrimony. Despite gaining the approval of the country's political elites on the Meech Lake Accord, a sudden surge of nationwide public opposition soon materialized about the fact that the treaty had been developed in secret, without public input or consultation. Following the election of several provincial governments that publicly opposed the deal, Meech Lake was defeated in 1990. Mulroney's second attempt to achieve a grand constitutional deal through a more inclusive process (one that included the use of a national referendum) once again ended with the defeat of the Charlottetown Accord in 1992. By the end of Mulroney's second term, it had become clear that the ills and grievances of the Canadian federation were unlikely to be solved by a grand constitutional bargain.

Mid-1990s — present: Pragmatism & compromise
The 1990s gave us the unusual style of federalist relations Canada has today. Central to this arrangement was the election of Jean Chrétien as prime minister in 1993. Chrétien was a fiercely pragmatic leader who had been a sitting MP since the early 1960s, and had seen firsthand over three decades the existential threat posed to Canada by poorly managed intergovernmental relations. Chrétien's instinct was to move away from the divisive constitutional exercises of his predecessor and instead focus on simply making the federation work through informal and ad hoc arrangements with the provinces. This inclination was almost certainly informed by the election of a fiercely anti-Ottawa government in Alberta under Ralph Klein, as well as a devoutly separatist Parti Québécois government in Québec under Jacques Parizeau — the latter of which once again brought Québec to the brink of secession in a narrow 1995 referendum.

But an equally important impetus for the change in federal–provincial relations throughout the 1990s mostly had to do with money. Declaring the federal debt to have reached emergency proportions, the Chrétien government pledged to undertake a determined effort to reduce the national deficit. In so doing, the government made use of the typical neoliberal tools of privatization, welfare service cuts, efficiency measures, etc. (see Chapter 6 for more on neoliberalism). But it also made use of a strategy that could be referred to as federal spending power in reverse, through which Ottawa dramatically pared-back transfer payments to the provinces for services like healthcare, education, and social assistance. Beginning in the mid-1990s, these payments were all rolled into the Canada Health & Social Transfer. In exchange for the significant reduction in money, the provinces were given fewer conditions on how they could spend it.

While the accommodation may have seemed insignificant or minor at the time, it actually marked the dawn of a new era in intergovernmental relations, as Ottawa's powers over social and economic policy were now radically reduced. Moreover, as provinces bore the brunt of public opposition and anxiety resulting from the significantly smaller social safety net, they found themselves without any obvious help or direction from the federal government. Indeed, in light of the new procedural accommodations and economic autonomy introduced during this period, whether they sought it or not, provincial governments were to become considerably more independent and powerful than at any other time in modern Canadian history.

Canadian Federalism & Climate Policy: Another *Very* Brief History

The tumultuous history described above laid the groundwork for the federalist structure under which Canada's climate policy has been developed over the past quarter century. Cameron and Simeon (2002) refer to this structure as "collaborative federalism" — a style of federalist relations where national policy is developed and implemented *not* by Ottawa dictating behaviour through its control over funding, but rather by the provincial, territorial, and federal governments working *collaboratively* in a somewhat ad hoc fashion as various issues arise.

Rather than cementing the rules of Canadian federalism in the rigid language of constitutional clauses, a series of mechanisms have been gradually established over the years (including, for example, federal–provincial conferences, interprovincial meetings, etc.) that attempt to create broad, consensual compromises between all the participants. Typically, these rough agreements are then expressed in the flexible and non-binding language of intergovernmental accords, declarations, and framework agreements, which set the broad parameters for national policy.

While collaborative federalism has undeniably helped to resolve several key issues that nearly drove Canada to the brink of fragmentation, it has nevertheless failed to address two crucial questions that have dogged national climate policy for decades. First, how can the country achieve *adequate* national standards (without pandering to the lowest common denominator) on a given issue when the provinces not only have widely divergent interests, but also the autonomy to act on those interests? And second, at the end of the day, who gets to define and enforce those standards?

This has indeed been the largest institutional hurdle for Canadian climate policy over the years. Instead of exercising its constitutional authority to act unilaterally on climate, Ottawa has simply encouraged the provinces to develop a national agreement, primarily through the use of the Canadian Council of Ministers of the Environment. While the Council gives the appearance of fairness and allows the provinces to maintain authority over the issue, its decisions are all consensus-based and completely non-binding. As a result, it has tended to produce lowest common denominator outcomes, typically dictated by high-emitting provinces like Alberta (Gordon and Macdonald 2011). Building on the work of Gordon and Macdonald (2011), the evolution of intergovernmental relations around climate in Canada can be roughly broken down into three eras.

1993–1998: Attempts at provincial coordination

As noted in Chapter 2, beginning in 1993, the Chrétien government sought to develop a national climate strategy using the Council of Ministers of Environment and Council of Energy Ministers. As each of these councils developed their own proposals, they were to be presented at annual meetings where the two councils met jointly — known as the Joint Meeting of Ministers (JMM). As one might have easily predicted, given the consensual nature of the process noted above, the result of JMM negotiations was an exceptionally weak strategy called the National Action Program on Climate Change, whose main policy instrument was the Voluntary Challenge and Emissions Registry. The program yielded no significant emissions cuts before its dissolution in the early 2000s. Worse still, the rationale of the JMM was dealt an existential blow in 1997, when, in the lead up to the Kyoto Conference, Chrétien unilaterally overruled the national emissions target agreed upon by the JMM and substituted his own.

1998–2006: Disintegration

In the wake of Chrétien's intervention at Kyoto, the JMM's credibility declined dramatically, leading to disengagement by both the provinces and Ottawa. Making matters worse, in 2002, Chrétien refused to seek permission from the JMM to ratify Kyoto, opting instead to do it unilaterally without input from the provinces. As a result, Alberta officially opted out of the JMM in late 2002, bringing about an unceremonious end to multilateral negotiations on climate. After Paul Martin failed to make significant progress on a series of bilateral deals with willing provinces, Stephen Harper officially ended Ottawa's participation in any intergovernmental negotiations on climate.

2006–2015: Provinces go it alone

With the election of the Harper government and the breakdown of the JMM process, numerous provinces opted to engage in their own climate policy experiments. Why did they decide to do this? As Houle, Lachapelle, and Rabe (2014) note, while unilateral action comes with its share of risks, most provinces had at least one of the following reasons for doing so. First, implementing your own climate policy can, obviously, be used to resolve growing calls for action by an angry electorate. Second, it can be used as a decoy to protect important local industries from international condemnation, and/or pre-empt the future imposition of federal climate regulations. And third, it can be used as an opportunity to capitalize on economic opportunities in emerging green-tech and financial markets. In the Canadian context, these factors can be seen in the moves made by the first three provinces to act on climate policy: Alberta, Québec, and British Columbia.

Alberta's decision to move forward with climate regulation has much to do with the second rationale noted above. In 2002, Ralph Klein's avowedly anti-climate government was concerned about two key threats to its oil sands industry. The first was growing international opposition to buying Alberta's oil, given that oil sand extraction is among the most environmentally damaging forms of energy production in the world.

And second, Klein was also fearful of the potential for unilateral imposition of federal climate regulation in the wake of Chrétien's ratification
of Kyoto. In an effort to defuse both of these threats, Klein sought to get
out ahead of the issue. Implemented in 2007, the Specified Gas Emitters
Regulation required that regulated facilities across the province reduce
their emissions intensity by 12 percent. Those that were unable to do so
were required to either pay $15 for every tonne of CO_2e over the limit,
purchase carbon offsets, or buy credits from another facility that managed to reduce emissions beyond their target. Klein's goal was two-fold.
First, he sought to give the impression to international buyers that, in fact,
Alberta's oil sands were responsible stewards of the environment, taking
adequate steps to regulate any potential ecological abuses. And second,
he sought to protect Alberta's oil and gas sector from pending federal
regulation given that, under Section 10 of the Canadian Environmental
Protection Act, a province can be exempt from federal regulation if they
are already taking action to achieve the same outcome (Houle, Lachapelle,
and Rabe 2014). The use of "intensity targets" instead of "absolute emissions caps" also provides a good sense of Klein's rationale. While absolute
caps require that overall emissions fall over time, intensity targets merely
require that the amount of emissions generated per barrel of oil declines.
Therefore, overall emissions are still allowed to rise indefinitely, as long
as efficiencies improve enough to meet the intensity target.

Québec began its efforts in 2002, as it signed agreements with various
domestic industries to commit these sectors to emissions cuts. The government's goals were once again two-fold, aiming to both appear responsive
to growing voter demand for climate action in the province, as well as
ensure recognition of early action from federal regulators. In 2007, Québec
adopted a small carbon tax amounting to $3 per tonne of CO_2. While the
tax was too small to generate any significant cuts, it nevertheless generated in excess of $200 million per year for a provincial green fund used
to finance climate action plans. Moreover, in 2009, the province joined
the Western Climate Initiative with several US states, which committed
members to reducing emissions 15 percent below 2005 levels by 2020
through a regional emissions trading system.

Finally, the BC experience is case of a government viewing climate
policy as an economic and political opportunity. In 2007, with polls indicating that environmental issues had topped the list of voter priorities in

the province, Gordon Campbell's Liberal party announced that climate leadership would be a central focus of the government. To that end, Campbell announced that his government would set a provincial emissions target of 33 percent below 2007 levels by 2020, enact a low-carbon fuel standard, and join the Western Climate Initiative. The next year, the Campbell government went a step further by becoming the first government in North America to adopt a revenue neutral system-wide carbon tax. Starting at $10 per tonne of CO_2, the tax is applied at the point of consumption on all fossil fuels consumed in the province and raises over $1 billion per year — which is used to offset personal and corporate taxes and reduce taxes for low-income earners (Harrison 2012a).

As Table 3.1 depicts, in the ensuing years several other provinces began their own climate policy experiments, with each government responding to the incentives noted above by introducing their own relatively light-touch initiatives.

Looking at the targets and measures noted in Table 3.1, it is clear that

TABLE 3.1 PROVINCIAL CLIMATE INITIATIVES, 2007–2015

PROVINCE	TARGET (ADJUSTED FOR 1990 BASELINE)	EXAMPLES OF MEASURES
BC	3% below 1990 by 2020	Carbon tax; subsidies/tax breaks for energy efficiency upgrades; Clean Energy Fund
Alberta	2.5% above 1990 by 2050	Intensity–based emissions levy
Saskatchewan	31% above 1990 by 2020	Clean technology fund; R&D funding
Manitoba	6% below 1990 by 2020	Coal fire plant phase out
Ontario	15% below 1990 by 2020	Coal fire plant phase out; tax breaks for energy efficiency upgrades; feed-in tariff
Québec	20% below 1990 by 2020	Carbon tax; green technology fund; tax incentives for energy efficiency upgrades
New Brunswick	10% below 1990 by 2020	Investments in renewables
Nova Scotia	10% below 1990 by 2020	Renewable energy standard; caps on utility emissions
PEI	10% below 1990 by 2020	Investments in renewables; vehicle emissions standards; tax incentives for efficiency upgrades
Newfoundland & Labrador	10% below 1990 by 2020	Renewable energy standard

none of this was ever going to lead to the type of rapid decarbonization of the Canadian economy that the science suggests is desperately needed. But it nevertheless bears asking, could this bizarre hodgepodge of provincial initiatives provide the seeds of a useful path forward?

While a patchwork of decentralized initiatives obviously provides no guarantee that national objectives will be met, the history of centralized initiatives over the past three decades has not been particularly heartening either. It is in this context that many commentators suggest that, while a patchwork approach is not perfect, it is surely better than total inaction (Bélanger 2011). Moreover, as noted above, there is potentially much to be learned from the various subnational experiments that could one day lead to a strong and effective national climate strategy.

Among the strongest argument for the provincial patchwork approach is the notion of the "California effect." For Vogel (1995), the California effect refers to the way that environmental regulations implemented in one powerful subnational jurisdiction can pressure industries that sell their products there to improve performance standards elsewhere. Over time, this can create an impetus to extend these standards to the national level — as was the case when California's ambitious 1966 auto emissions standards were eventually implemented by the federal Congress.

The California effect occurred again when California became the first US state to create GHG emissions standards for cars in 2004. Over the following years, fourteen other states (which, combined with California, had a total population of over 120 million) indicated that they would match California's standard. The Obama administration subsequently noted that it only made sense to extend this standard nationwide and soon implemented legislation to that effect. Over the following years, California's ambitious Global Warming Solutions Act of 2006 (which set a target of returning emissions to 1990 levels by 2020 — a target which has now been achieved) inspired dozens of other states to adopt targets of their own. Indeed, the California effect shows that one large and ambitious subnational government can create a powerful momentum for broader change by reducing competitive impacts, providing a proven policy map, and helping to coordinate the strategies of like-minded states (Harrison 2012b).

At the same time, however, others believe that the patchwork approach ought to be viewed with skepticism, especially in Canada. Harrison (2013) is quick to point out that, although provincial initiatives have been a welcome partial substitute for federal action, they are nevertheless still *just a partial* substitute. As she notes, while there have been some instances of admirable provincial leadership, it has tended to emerge very selectively in the provinces that already have some of the lowest emissions and least fossil fuel-intensive economies. For example, the two standout leaders, BC and Québec, already had per-capita emissions that were a mere fraction of those found in places like Alberta and Saskatchewan — both of whom resisted any serious action for decades. And while provincial leaders in Canada have, to a certain extent, engaged in policy coordination on climate, they have not followed their US counterparts in lobbying the federal government to extend those standards nationally. Indeed, in contrast to California's lawsuits to demand federal regulations from the US government, Québec (one of only two provinces to support the ratification of Kyoto in the early 2000s) actually supported Alberta's position that federal climate regulation should *not* be imposed on the provinces unilaterally. In Canada, it appears that the principles of provincial autonomy and self-determination carry more weight than those of climate protection.

2015–2019: Back to the national coordination future

Justin Trudeau came into office with the goal of finally achieving a comprehensive nation-wide climate agreement between the provinces. As noted in Chapter 2, he initially took on this task with something that Jean Chrétien and Paul Martin could only have dreamed about in the 1990s and 2000s: sympathetic, centrist governments in power in Alberta, BC, Ontario, Québec, New Brunswick, Nova Scotia, Prince Edward Island, Newfoundland & Labrador, Nunavut, Yukon, and the Northwest Territories. Indeed, as noted above, in the Canadian system, federalism can actually become extremely beneficial for climate policy in the *exceptionally* unlikely event that pro-climate governments come to power in effectively every major jurisdiction. And, with the exception of Saskatchewan and Manitoba, this is what happened in 2015. As a result, the achievement of an intergovernmental treaty in 2016 actually turned out to be reasonably straightforward. As we'll discuss in Chapter 6, the big question moving forward is whether or not this deal can be sustained as right-wing governments inevitably return to power, particularly in crucial provinces like Alberta and Ontario.

Canadian Cities & Climate Governance

There is yet another layer to the intergovernmental complexity around climate policy. Around the world, towns and cities have also begun to take on prominent roles in climate governance, acting individually within their own jurisdictions, as well as collectively through a variety of transnational governance networks (Bulkeley and Betsill 2003). Emerging as a response to the failure of many national governments to address the problem, these new forms of "networked urban governance" have managed to promote significant emissions reductions through inter-city coordination efforts (Kern and Bulkeley 2009).

While municipal climate governance is not a suitable proxy for a national strategy, cities are potentially useful for a few key reasons. First, and most obvious, municipalities are the source of up to 80 percent of GHG emissions worldwide — because, obviously, this is where most people and businesses are located (Dodman and Satterthwaite 2009). Second, they are the place where the impacts of climate change are most tangibly felt — in terms of threats to vulnerable communities, impacts of extreme weather events, infrastructural issues, or public health. And finally, as is often the case in municipal governance, cities tend to have the strongest impulse to act, given that they feel more direct pressure from their citizens than do national and/or provincial governments (Gore 2010). These factors have even greater weight in Canada, where over 80 percent of the population lives in cities, and municipalities have direct influence over numerous GHG emitting activities and issues (for example, transportation, building codes, urban development and planning, infrastructure, etc.) (Gordon 2015b).

In this context, Canadian cities have a potentially enormous role to play in pushing the country toward decarbonization. And yet, as we will see below, this potential has, for a few key reasons, gone unfulfilled over the decades.

Partners for climate protection

According to Kern and Bulkeley (2009), the greatest potential for cities to have an impact on decarbonization comes from being part of a broader network of municipalities — one that can generate aggregate emissions reductions that are greater than the sum of its parts. To do so, they suggest that an effective network must be able to play a few key roles, including communicate key information about governance initiatives to its members, provide funding and coordination for various projects, and provide continuous benchmarks and other incentives to keep its members engaged.

In Canada, the first inter-city network to try to play this role was an international one called the Cities for Climate Protection. Formed in 1993, the network established the goal of cutting GHG emissions from its member cities by 20 percent below 2000 levels within ten years of joining the network. Soon after its formation, however, the network decentralized into a series of regional ones, which in Canada became the Partners for Climate Protection (PCP). Over the ensuing years, the PCP's membership grew to include 247 Canadian municipalities as of 2014, encompassing over 80 percent of the country's population (Gordon 2015b).

In line with Kern and Bulkeley's requirements noted above, the PCP developed a few key steering mechanisms to promote successful action by its members. In terms of hard resources, the PCP aims to provide a series of technical tools to its member cities (including emissions inventory software, documents to assist in the development of specific policies, and workshops for municipal policymakers), as well as disseminate up-to-date knowledge about best practices, new opportunities, and policy ideas. At a more intangible level, the PCP also tries to socialize its members to the idea that they have a significant role to play in climate governance (mostly by educating them about the economic and livability benefits of climate action), and providing some suggested targets and milestones to live up to (Gordon 2015b).

A well-intentioned failure?

In many important respects, the PCP has been successful. Not only has it brought hundreds of cities within its orbit over the years, but it has played a crucial role in educating municipal governments across the country about potential climate policy options at their disposal, largely by disseminating an inventory of the more than eight hundred projects taken up by cities across the network.

At the same time, however, the PCP has left much to be desired. As Gordon (2015b) notes, while the PCP has tried to be the "centre of the wheel" and engage Canadian cities in the most innovative and effective forms of climate governance possible, its capacity to do so has remained extremely limited. With a miniscule annual budget of just $150,000 (and only one permanent staff member), the PCP's ability to "network the network" is effectively zero. This is plain to see in the services it offers. While it has compiled and circulated a series of best practice studies and project ideas, it provides no networking platform for peer-to-peer information flow, and thus links between the PCP and the cities are rather weak. In Toronto, for example, relevant city officials interviewed about their experience with climate governance initiatives were unaware of any resources offered by the PCP, and considered it immaterial to their work (Gordon 2015b).

As a result of being so under-resourced, the PCP has engaged neither "ambitious" nor "beginner" cities across the country. As Gordon notes,

> The PCP was unable to keep Toronto engaged in the network through the late 1990s and early to mid 2000s, when Toronto was an active, ambitious, and aggressive leader in local climate governance. Absent opportunities for city leadership within the network, ambitious cities such as Toronto are presented with limited benefits from active participation in the PCP and can be expected to direct their efforts elsewhere. In Winnipeg, while there is considerable evidence that the PCP was able to support and influence the city at early stages of engagement, the governance mechanisms employed by the network vis-à-vis the city (the weak emphasis on targets, financial supports unlinked to performance outcomes) appear to have enabled this early pioneering impulse to be derailed once political support waned. We see, in other words, a network that has been unable to either keep an ambitious city within its orbit or hold a less ambitious city to its commitments. (Gordon 2015b: 12)

The PCP's relative inefficacy has much to do with the nature of inter-governmental relations in Canada — specifically the jurisdictional weakness of cities within the Constitution. Indeed, throughout its text, the Constitution says very little about municipalities, beyond the fact that the provinces have full authority to legislate over them. This, in turn, has led to the famous idea that cities are merely "creatures of the provinces," and that they have no inherent capacities (or even, quite literally, a legal right to exist). As a result, municipal governments have historically had a tumultuous relationship with the provincial and federal governments when it comes to money, resources, autonomy, and policy development. They are viewed by the upper levels of government as, in effect, policy *takers* not policy *makers*.

This state of affairs has had a crippling impact on both municipal climate governance and the networks that aim to develop it. The PCP desperately needs strong and consistent financial resources in order to be effective. But, aside from a small amount of private sector funding, most of the money must come from Ottawa or the provinces — neither of whom have ever taken a serious interest in viewing the cities as partners in climate governance. This is somewhat surprising given that, in many respects, cities could actually be the answer that climate advocates in Ottawa have been looking for all along. Moving the focus to municipal initiatives (and providing adequate federal grants and incentives for cities to do so) could effectively leapfrog any stalemates between Ottawa and the provinces, and develop consequential initiatives in the places where the majority of emissions are generated.

Implications & Lessons for Climate Advocates

While climate advocates probably cannot hope to broadly reform the current structure of Canadian federalism, they can nevertheless try to work cleverly within its confines, both exploiting opportunities where they exist and learning how to navigate potential pitfalls. Among the most important takeaways here is a knowledge and appreciation of the California effect. As described above, this phenomenon occurs when one state/province within a federated country develops innovative policies in a given area, which then creates momentum for similar policies to spread across the country — perhaps even to the federal level. The key takeaway from the California effect is that, while it remains crucial to demand that national leaders implement strong climate policies and enforce minimum federal standards, it is arguably more important (given the nature of Canadian federalism) to place relentless pressure on provincial governments to become climate champions. It is worth noting, moreover, that the California effect is most successful when the pioneering provinces are those with the largest populations and economies (as, indeed, California is in the US), suggesting that, while strong policies are needed in every single province and territory, the biggest payoffs will come from pressuring Ontario, Québec, BC, and Alberta to go above and beyond. For their part, federal policymakers can accelerate and bolster the California effect by creating policies that encourage a race-to-the-top dynamic (in the form of subsidies, infrastructure investments, and other incentives) that will compel provinces to compete to have the best policies.

In terms of pitfalls, arguably the most important thing that a knowledge of federalism can teach climate advocates is the dangers associated with concentrated regional costs. As noted above, if powerful provinces are forced to disproportionately endure the negative impacts of national climate policy, the nature of Canadian federalism allows them to effectively scuttle Ottawa's plans. As we saw in Chapter 2, Alberta has, in defense of its oil and gas industry, played this role for the better part of three decades. Fortunately, however, there are some straightforward policies that climate advocates can push for to alleviate these impacts. The German case provides perhaps the most instructive example, where individual states with large coal industries (for example, Saarland and North Rhine Westphalia) received federal assistance to help transition the state's economy and workers towards a secure and prosperous post-coal future. These policies consisted of incentives to locate new clean-tech industries in these states, investments in technology-hubs to usher in a robust high-tech/knowledge-based economy, large environmental and infrastructure projects aimed at cleaning up former mine sites, and investments designed to enhance tourism in the region. For the workers themselves, governments provided funding to bolster early-retirement packages for older coal workers, voluntary redundancy and transition payment schemes, and qualification training for displaced workers. The result was that these states were able to successfully transition more than 100,000 former coal workers and build modern economies capable of thriving in the twenty-first century. If these types of strategies can be applied in Canadian provinces that feel threatened by climate policy, then their penchant to thwart a national strategy can be significantly reduced.

A final key takeaway from this discussion of federalism has to do with the invaluable role that cities and towns can play. As noted above, Canadian cities are home to over 80 percent of the country's residents and carbon emissions, and have direct influence over numerous GHG emitting activities (including building codes, urban planning, public transit, infrastructure, and even agriculture/land management). Municipal governments, moreover, tend to be more susceptible to direct pressure from voters. In this context, climate advocates need to devote increased time and energy to pressuring city councils to take decisive action, and demand that Ottawa devote more resources to assisting cities directly.

INSTITUTION #2: FIRST PAST THE POST ELECTORAL SYSTEM

Since Confederation in 1867, all elections in Canada have made use of one particular system to select representatives and establish governments. This system is commonly referred to as First Past the Post (FPTP). The use of FPTP in Canada is a legacy of British colonialism, with this system having been left behind in most of the UK's former colonies that moved toward democratic elections. Over the years, however, many of those countries have gradually abandoned FPTP (for reasons we'll explore below) in favour of alternative systems. As of 2017, Canada is one of the only remaining industrialized countries in the world still using FPTP (see Figure 3.1).

Under this system, the country is divided into numerous ridings or electorates (as of 2015, there were 338 federal ridings across Canada), and each riding is permitted to select a local Member of Parliament (MP) to represent it in the legislature. When entering the voting booth, voters are presented with the extremely simple task of ticking the box next to their preferred candidate's name. The candidate who gets the most votes in each riding wins the seat, and the party with the most seats is typically invited to form the government. This stands in contrast to Proportional Representation systems, where voters may have to choose a "party list" (or select a number of "secondary preference" candidates),

FIGURE 3.1 FIRST PAST THE POST AROUND THE WORLD

Source: Wikimedia Commons 2019

and each party is awarded seats based on the percentage of the popular vote they received.

As we'll see below, the primary virtue of FPTP is its overwhelming simplicity — it is quick, easy to understand, and leaves little room for confusion or complication. This contrasts with many proportional representation systems, which voters often find slightly more complicated and time-consuming. But while FPTP has certain undeniable advantages over alternative systems, it has nevertheless created a formidable barrier to climate action in Canada over the past three decades. As we'll see, this system has served to dampen the expression of public concern about climate change and the environment, creating a structure where governments and politicians are often not compelled to listen to environmentally-minded voters.

Advantages of First Past the Post

FPTP has several apparent benefits that have helped maintain its relative popularity over the decades. The first and most obvious, as just noted, is its simplicity. Especially when compared with some of the more complex proportional representation systems (discussed below), the average voter easily understands FPTP — a valid vote requires one check mark beside the preferred candidate's name, and the candidate with the most votes wins the seat, end of story. Second, FPTP is very quick and cheap. While some alternative systems can take weeks of tabulating and negotiation to declare a government, FPTP is easy to count, and the winner of each seat (and the government broadly) can usually be declared within a couple hours of the polls closing. Third, FPTP systems have historically been less

TABLE 3.2 SEAT BONUSES IN RECENT FEDERAL ELECTIONS

ELECTION	WINNER	% OF VOTE	% OF SEATS
2015	Liberal	39%	54%
2011	Conservative	39%	54%
2008	Conservative	37%	46%
2006	Conservative	36%	40%
2004	Liberal	36%	43%
2000	Liberal	40%	57%
1997	Liberal	38%	51%
1993	Liberal	41%	60%
1988	PC	43%	57%

likely to allow extremist parties to win seats. Given that such parties are required to win a plurality of votes in numerous different ridings across the country, they are more likely to be completely shut out of the legislature than under a proportional representation system. And finally, FPTP tends to create stable, single-party governments that are able to efficiently enact their agenda, without having to rely on coalition partners. This is a result of the system's tendency to generate so-called seat bonuses for the largest party. As Table 3.2 depicts, in the 2015 election, Justin Trudeau's Liberal Party won just 39 percent of the vote, but was granted 54 percent of the parliament's seats. Moreover, since the end of the Second World War, Canada has had twelve majority governments, despite the fact that only two parties have actually won a majority of the national vote during that time. This creates a situation where smaller parties remain quite weak and coalition governments are extremely rare (indeed, Canada has never had a coalition government at the federal level).

Disadvantages of First Past the Post

All of that said, however, FPTP has numerous shortcomings as well — some of which have proved disastrous for climate policy in Canada. The first is that, as noted above, individual MPs (and, by extension, entire governments) can get elected with relatively small amounts of popular support. Unlike proportional representation systems, which aim to ensure that each party's percentage of seats in parliament is commensurate with the percentage of the popular vote they garnered, FPTP requires only that a candidate receive a plurality of votes in their district. This creates a situation where seats can be won simply because numerous parties with similar platforms can end up splitting the vote and allowing a considerably less popular party to capture the seat. This has been a recurring theme in Canadian federal politics over the years, most recently with parties on the centre left (e.g., the Liberals, NDP, Greens, and Bloc Québécois) allowing Conservatives to win numerous progressive/centrist districts.

Second, and very much related to the first point, FPTP creates a situation where a large percentage of the total votes cast is effectively wasted. Unlike a proportional representation system (where every vote contributes to the final composition of the government) any vote in a FPTP system that does not go to the winning candidate ultimately counts for nothing. In the 2015 federal election, for example, of the more than seventeen million votes cast across the country, more than nine million were wasted because they were cast for losing candidates. This situation depresses voter turnout (particularly among younger Canadians), as it contributes to the perception that one's vote does not make a difference.

Finally, as noted above, FPTP tends to marginalize smaller parties. Unlike proportional representation systems (where a smaller party that receives, for example, 10 percent of the vote wins 10 percent of the parliamentary seats, and can perhaps become part of a governing coalition), FPTP creates a situation where, unless support is tightly concentrated in specific ridings, smaller parties are often unable to win any seats.

First Past the Post & Climate Policy

Data on the relationship between electoral systems and climate policy suggest that countries with proportional representation systems tend to have much more ambitious action than those with FPTP — though key exceptions do exist (Christoff and Eckersley 2011). Indeed, since they are able to give much greater expression to minority viewpoints, proportional representation systems create a situation where politicians and governments must be more attuned to the views of environmental voters, even if ecological issues are not a concern for median voters. This is particularly the case when it comes to younger Canadians, who overwhelmingly believe in climate change and want to see action. Studies from around the world show that proportional representation systems not only have much higher voter turnout overall, but, in particular, have much higher youth participation — thus creating more space for environmental issues like climate change (Norris 1997; Karp and Banducci 1999; Milner 2009).

By contrast, since FPTP systems tend to lock minority viewpoints out of power and depress youth turnout, it creates a situation where an issue like climate change has to gain immense salience for a majority of voters before governments will seriously pursue it. This has been the case in Canada for decades, as governments at both the federal and provincial levels focus their attention on the concerns of median voters, and green voters tend to be marginalized.

Indeed, a big part of the explanation for Ottawa's idleness on climate can be found in the ideologies of the country's two major parties and the way that FPTP entrenches these positions. For its part, the Liberal party managed to dominate national politics throughout the post-war period by carefully tailoring its positions to fit current political fashions and trying to maintain the largest possible coalition. With no first-principle ideological commitment to environmentalism, the party has only ever taken decisive action on ecological issues during the brief moments when public interest rises among their coalition of voters. Although the Conservative party is clearly more ideological, that ideology is firmly bent towards favouring economic growth and resource extraction over environmental protection. While Stephen Harper demonstrated in 2007 that he too could be pressured by growing public support for climate action, he quickly backed off as public interest faded. With a similar pattern observed in most provinces over the past thirty years, the result is that, with a few momentary exceptions, environmental issues have always struggled to secure the support of the country's major parties.

First Past the Post & Green Party Representation

The experience of the Canadian Green Party since its founding provides a clear example of the frustrations FPTP creates. As seen in Table 3.3, though the party has, in recent election cycles, tended to garner roughly 5 percent of the vote in federal elections, it has only managed to win a single seat on two occasions — both of which were in the party leader's home riding. Polling between elections suggests that support for the party often sits around 10 percent, but, in a classic case of vote splitting, many sympathetic voters strategically opt for another progressive party that might have a better chance of defeating the Conservative candidate (e.g., the Liberals, NDP, or Bloc Québécois). As Table 3.3 also shows, under a proportional representation system, assuming the threshold was not prohibitively high, the Greens would have had a very respectable presence in the House of Commons in each election since 2004, and, in the minority governments that ruled between 2004–2011, could have found themselves

TABLE 3.3 THE CANADIAN GREEN PARTY & RECENT FEDERAL ELECTIONS

ELECTION	POPULAR VOTE	SEATS WON UNDER FPTP	SEATS POTENTIALLY WON UNDER PR
2004	4.3%	0	18
2006	4.4%	0	18
2008	6.7%	0	22
2011	3.9%	1	17
2015	3.4%	1	16

TABLE 3.4 GREEN PARTIES & RECENT PROVINCIAL ELECTIONS

PROVINCE/ELECTION	POPULAR VOTE	SEATS WON UNDER FPTP	SEATS POTENTIALLY WON UNDER PR
Ontario, 2018	5%	1	7
BC, 2017	17%	3	15
Manitoba, 2016	5%	0	3
PEI, 2015	11%	1	3
New Brunswick, 2014	7%	1	4

in a governing coalition or holding the balance of power.

As Table 3.4 shows, the story is the same at the provincial level, where several prominent Green parties have been effectively locked out of their respective legislatures despite winning significant percentages of the vote — and polling significantly better than their actual vote percentage in the run-up to the election.

An instructive example of the party's potential under a different system can be found in New Zealand, which switched from FPTP to proportional representation after holding a national referendum on the issue in 1993. Prior to the switch, the New Zealand Greens, like their Canadian counterparts, typically won around 5 percent of the national vote and yet were shut out of the legislature. However, in each of the past seven national elections, the party has managed to win anywhere from six to fourteen seats, allowing it to negotiate important environmental concessions from the governing party.

First Past the Post & Youth/Progressive Turnout

Given that younger Canadians (particularly the 18–35-year-old demographic) tend to express the most concern and passion for environmental issues, their participation in the electoral process is crucial for getting governments to take serious action on climate. And yet, thanks in large part to FPTP, this demographic is the least likely to take part. Indeed, in recent federal elections the turnout of 18–35-year-olds has averaged a measly 37 percent (Barnes 2011). Much the same can be said of progressive/left-leaning voters, who are also crucial for compelling governments to take climate seriously and yet are significantly less likely to participate than more conservative/right-leaning voters (Karp and Banducci 1999).

How does FPTP suppress the turnout of these groups? In general, FPTP actually decreases the turnout of *every* demographic across the board — and, indeed, jurisdictions around the world with proportional representation have significantly higher voter turnouts overall (Norris 1997). FPTP does this by, as noted above, generating large volumes of wasted votes; decreasing the number of parties, candidates, and choices; and making elections less competitive — all of which leaves voters with a higher feeling of apathy about elections, and the belief that, unless they live in a swing riding, their vote doesn't count for much. But while this feeling is present in every demographic, a study of participation levels for voters between 18–29 years of age in fifteen countries found that the youth turnout rate was, on average, 12 percentage points lower in FPTP countries, as compared with proportional representation ones (Milner 2009). The data suggest that, while FPTP depresses voter turnout across the board, it is most pronounced in demographics that are already quite vulnerable to abstaining. This applies to progressive voters as well. In their 1999 study, Karp and Banducci found that, as New Zealand switched to a proportional representation system, progressive voters suddenly became significantly more likely to participate. They suggest this occurred because not only did progressive voters feel more encouraged that their vote would matter, but political parties had much stronger incentives to mobilize every demographic of voters, as there were no longer any wasted votes.

The good news is that, according to a 2016 Environics poll, a solid plurality of Canadians (41 percent) supports the idea of scrapping FPTP at the federal level and replacing it with an alternative system (see Figure 3.2). The bad news is that, not only is there no clear preference on what

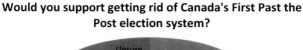
FIGURE 3.2 NATIONAL SUPPORT FOR FIRST PAST THE POST

Would you support getting rid of Canada's First Past the Post election system?

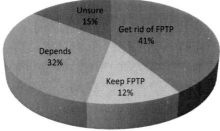

Source: adapted from Angus Reid 2016

FIGURE 3.3 PREFERRED ALTERNATIVES TO FIRST PAST THE POST

If you seek an end to FPTP, what should replace it?

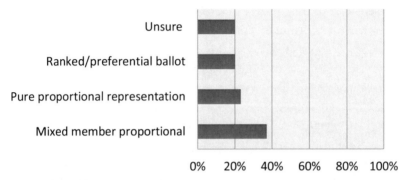

Source: adapted from Angus Reid 2016

that replacement should be (which presumably will be a requirement if a referendum on electoral reform is to succeed — see Figure 3.3), but the task of implementing such a change is ceaselessly in the hands of a government that recently received a healthy seat bonus from the FPTP system. In this context, the incentives for a sitting government to undertake such a potentially complicated shift (particularly one that is only likely to benefit opposition parties) is quite small. It is in this context that, despite Justin Trudeau's 2015 campaign pledge to implement a shift to a proportional representation system, the Prime Minister staunchly refused to do so upon taking office, even after receiving a strong recommendation from his own Special Committee on Electoral Reform that proportional representation made the most sense for the Canadian political system.

Implications & Lessons for Climate Advocates

The key takeaway from this discussion is clear: climate advocates must demand an immediate end to FPTP at the federal, provincial, and municipal levels. It is no coincidence that all of Canada's fellow industrialized countries (save for the US and UK) have moved beyond this antiquated legacy of British colonial rule. Put plainly, FPTP is unfair and unrepresentative. It leaves millions of Canadians unrepresented in legislatures across the country and typically renders the majority of votes cast in any election wasted. Environmental voters, in particular, have suffered at the hands of this institution for decades, forced to watch as their views and opinions are swept aside by false-majority governments that have no incentive to listen to them. At the risk of over-simplifying, one could argue that this is the single most important thing that climate advocates in Canada should be fighting for right now. Under a system of proportional representation, environmental and progressive voters will finally be appropriately represented in parliament, and governments will be forced to take their demands seriously.

INSTITUTION #3: THE CANADIAN LEGAL SYSTEM & ABORIGINAL TITLE

It may seem odd to think it, but some of the largest sources of Canada's GHG emissions are technically unlawful, and if the Canadian legal system actually functioned properly, they would likely need to be shut down immediately. This is because, according to the Constitution, massive fossil fuel megaprojects all across Canada (but particularly the tar sands in Alberta) have proceeded for decades in violation of basic constitutional statutes around Aboriginal land title.

Indeed, First Nations peoples hold historical treaties that cover large swaths of Canadian territory from coast to coast to coast. Their rights and jurisdiction over these lands (and decision-making powers concerning them) are fully enshrined in Section 35 of the Constitution Act of 1982. The Supreme Court of Canada has, moreover, determined that the government has enduring obligations to reconcile the settlement and development of *all lands* with Indigenous rights and title. Indeed, it is on this basis that Ottawa has distinct, structural, legal obligations to respect Indigenous control over their lands — particularly when it comes to high-risk fossil fuel projects and pipelines that pose a serious risk to their lands, waters, health, and safety.

Yet, as we'll see below, as an institution, the Canadian legal system has never managed to enforce this basic provision. This owes, in large part, to the fact that the system has never fully reconciled the place of First Nations peoples within Canadian jurisprudence, or the fact that they constitute sovereign governments and jurisdictions outside the Canadian legal order. Thus, lacking any committed effort to rectify this situation, it has proved relatively easy to openly violate Section 35 of the Constitution and engage in illegal fossil fuel development on their lands.

"Field Notes from a Catastrophe"

The story of the Lubicon Cree in Northern Alberta is emblematic of this situation. Located on more than 10,000 km² of land that was once pristine boreal forest, clean rivers, and unspoiled wetlands, the Lubicon Cree have seen their territory undergo a horrific transformation in light of oil and gas development over the past several decades. Importantly, this has all occurred without their consent or recognition of their land rights. Indeed, at the time of writing, there are several thousand technically illegal oil and gas wells located inside their territory, with 70 percent of their remaining territory released (without consent) for future development by the federal government (Laboucan-Massimo 2014).

The results of this development have been devastating for the Lubicon Cree. At the same time that billions of dollars in oil and gas revenue has been extracted from their land, the community has come to live in some of the worst poverty in the country, as their once bountiful territory has been converted to an industrial wasteland, and relentless fossil fuel projects have gradually destroyed the lands, watersheds, and wildlife on which they rely. As a result, their previous self-sufficiency has been replaced by heightened dependence on lacklustre social services, while their community has been forced to experience some of the highest rates of cancer and respiratory illness in the country as a consequence of the industrial toxins being released into their air and water. The government's treatment of this community has been condemned by the United Nations on multiple occasions, with the international community calling for a moratorium on fossil fuel development within their territory.

Unfortunately, their story is not an isolated example. The Beaver Lake Cree live in Treaty Six territory in Northern Alberta, where a bitumen extraction process known as Steam Assisted Gravity Drainage has decimated the previously unspoiled lands on which they relied. Steam Assisted Gravity Drainage is a particularly brutal environmental process that, to date, has seen an estimated 1.5 million litres of bitumen emulsion seep to the land's surface, thus contaminating groundwater and plants, and decimating the fish and wildlife upon which these people have depended for literally thousands of years (Lameman 2014). Where there was once self-sufficiency, there is now endemic boil-water advisories, and a stream of residents being airlifted to urban medical centres for sickness resulting from drinking contaminated water.

Once again, in creating this catastrophe, the Canadian government has refused to acknowledge that this Indigenous community has *full legal rights* over this land, as per an 1876 Treaty between the British Crown and First Nations Peoples. In violation of this treaty, Ottawa has not followed its legal requirement to obtain the free, prior, and informed consent of the Beaver Lake Cree, nor has it lived up to Article 32 of the United Nations Declaration on the Rights of Indigenous Peoples, which states that Indigenous peoples have a right to determine and develop priorities for the use of their territories and resources. To date, more than 19,000 permits have been granted (without permission) to oil companies from around the world, creating a situation where 84% of the Beaver Lake Cree Nation's 38,972 km^2 of territory has been filled with unauthorized oil and gas well sites.

Unfortunately, the cases of the Lubicon Cree and Beaver Lake Cree are just two small examples of a much wider catastrophe. In all of the Indigenous lands surrounding the mammoth tar sands mines and processing facilities, a similar story can be heard. Each year greater swaths of lands are destroyed by mines the size of entire cities, more industry access roads displace vulnerable wildlife, more industrial plants toxify the air and surrounding plant life, more lakes are drained, more toxic tailing ponds are created, and more oil spills degrade the soil — all of which leaves these communities with feelings of sadness, anger, hopelessness, despair, and rage. And while the oil industry claims that mined lands can be reclaimed and restored within a few decades, these communities are well aware that people and wildlife cannot simply return to land that has been stripped of all of its complex, life-giving elements and filled with toxic tailings (Cardinal 2014).

While the situation faced by Indigenous communities in Northern Alberta is particularly horrific, similar stories of unauthorized development, treaty violations, and environmental destruction occur every day all across Canada. Whether it's uranium mining or crude oil extraction in Saskatchewan, diamond mining in Ontario, natural gas fracking in New Brunswick, mineral mining throughout the three territories, or the numerous communities across British Columbia who have had pipelines introduced into their lands without permission, we see a legal system in Canada which is unable to uphold the basic constitutional rights of Indigenous peoples (Cardinal 2014).

What Does All of This Mean?

It is important to remember that, when Indigenous rights were recognized and enshrined in the Canadian Constitution, the Constitution did not thereby "create" them out of thin air. Indigenous peoples have lived in the territory that would come to be known as Canada for tens of thousands of years. Throughout this time, they lived as organized societies with their own laws — laws which existed thousands of years before the Canadian Constitution was written, thousands of years before the government of Canada was established, and thousands of years before the British Crown was created. Indeed, as a concept, Aboriginal rights were merely *framed* within Canadian jurisprudence to account for Indigenous legal orders that preceded the Canadian government and continue to remain outside of it. Put simply, these legal obligations stem from treaties signed between *sovereign nations*. When Indigenous communities entered into them, they were never agreeing to surrender their lands or cede their rights over them. They believed that these were honest treaties that could never be broken and would be upheld as an everlasting agreement of peace and friendship between sovereign nations.

All of this is worth underscoring because it means that there are solid constitutional grounds on which to stop the fossil fuel megaprojects that have not only destroyed massive swaths of Indigenous lands, but have also stood as one of Canada's largest contributions to global climate change — indeed, oil and gas process emissions (i.e. *not* including consumption) represent a quarter of all Canadian emissions. If large portions of tar sands development are recognized to be unconstitutional, many current and future projects would no longer be able to proceed without the permission of these communities. This would set a precedent for other Indigenous communities across the country, who could likewise prevent further impositions upon their territories. In short, this would constitute perhaps the most radical upending of Canadian climate and energy policy imaginable today.

This is obviously an unnerving prospect for the Canadian and Alberta governments, both of whom rely extensively on fossil fuel extraction to generate economic growth, jobs, and tax revenue (see Chapter 4 for more on this). As a result, ignoring and marginalizing Aboriginal title has stood as a key objective for governments, along with expanding pipeline capacity and streamlining environmental regulations on behalf of the oil and gas industry.

Emblematic of this effort is the government's Joint Review Process, which is the mechanism by which Indigenous communities are supposed to be consulted about industrial development on their lands. For many communities, however, the Joint Review Process is a tokenistic sham which, far from empowering Indigenous peoples and giving them control over their territories, has served to actively muscle them out of the process entirely. Among a long list of complaints about the process, critics note that the Joint Review Process was unilaterally imposed on Indigenous peoples without their consent, fundamentally does not respect Indigenous jurisdiction over their lands, did not use meaningful consultation to develop the terms of reference for the process, shows a general lack of respect for culturally relevant concerns around development projects, and serves to prevent communities from exercising autonomy over their lands by luring them into an endless labyrinth of bureaucracy that never seems to yield positive results (McCreary 2014).

Implications & Lessons for Climate Advocates

The key takeaway for climate advocates is that, as all other aspects of Canadian climate policy have failed to yield sufficient results, the constitutional rights of Indigenous peoples have increasingly become a vital framework to articulate the possibility of real policy change. Put simply, an honest reading of the Canadian Constitution tells us that much of the country's fossil fuel projects are not strictly legal, and climate advocates must not be shy about exposing and underscoring this fact.

It is also important to remind non-Indigenous Canadians that they too are a party to these treaties. This means that these agreements have not only been written in your name, but they have been abused in your name as well. As a result, it is the responsibility of all Canadians to demand that their governments respect Indigenous rights as outlined in the Canadian Constitution, numerous court rulings, and the UN Declaration on the Rights of Indigenous Peoples. It means demanding that federal and provincial governments obtain the *full consent* of Indigenous communities and stop violently forcing unauthorized mines and pipelines upon Aboriginal lands.

It also means no longer assuming that the Canadian Constitution is a completely sacrosanct document, or that the legal system can always be trusted to uphold its key tenets. Indeed, it is worth acknowledging that, while Indigenous rights are meant to be protected under Section 35 of the Constitution, this section was only added in at the last minute, and was done so unwillingly and under duress. When drafting the Constitution Act, Pierre Trudeau's government initially sought to omit Indigenous rights from the document as a last-ditch effort to force Aboriginal assimilation after the failure of the infamous 1969 White Paper on the status of Indigenous peoples. It was only after mass mobilizations by Indigenous communities (and sympathetic non-Indigenous Canadians) that Section 35 was reluctantly added. And, as we saw above, since then, governments have sought to ignore and dismiss it whenever it has suited them. This makes Section 35 a rather unique component of the Constitution — one that was only *added* under extreme pressure, and will only be *applied and enforced* under extreme pressure as well.

Fortunately, efforts to ignore this section of the Constitution have not gone completely unnoticed, and a growing resistance movement has materialized in recent years. One of the leading forces of this movement has been Indigenous communities located along existing and planned oil pipeline corridors, whose sovereignty is imminently threatened by these projects. Their resistance has taken many forms to date, including the famed Idle No More movement that drew international attention and condemnation of Canada's treatment of these communities, as well as the Treaty Alliance Against Tar Sands Expansion — comprised of 150 Indigenous Nations in Canada and the US — which has launched numerous legal actions to date against pipeline projects. As this resistance network has grown and evolved, it has attracted the attention of climate activists who, rightly, have acknowledged that Indigenous rights may be the most powerful form of environmental law in Canada, as they hold the key to preventing further expansion of the tar sands and other fossil fuel megaprojects.

CHAPTER 4

ECONOMIC INTERESTS

To really understand the history and trajectory of Canadian climate policy, it is crucial to appreciate the economic interests of the country's governments (both federal and provincial), businesses, and workers. In a capitalist society like Canada's, the economic objectives of these three groups tend, in most cases, to dictate the direction of policy — or at least structure the political battles that determine its outcome.

Interests can be broadly defined as the "tangible, material interests of society's principal actors, whether conceived as individuals or groups" (Hall 1997: 176). Though not without their critics, "Rational Choice" theorists argue that an understanding of the interests of these individuals and groups can allow researchers to model, predict, and understand their decisions. As long as the individual or group is rational and not random or impulsive (that is to say their decisions are self-interested, goal-oriented, reflective, and consistent over time and in different situations), researchers can infer back from observed behaviour to understand the interests and preferences that drive their decisions.

As we will see in this chapter, the three main interest groups being explored (governments, businesses, and workers) all have a reasonably consistent set of objectives and concerns when it comes to climate policy. The dynamism and turmoil of Canadian climate policy derives, in many ways, from the enormous variation in interests both within and between these groups, as well as the marginal position that the environment enjoys in each group's hierarchy of interests.

ECONOMIC INTEREST GROUP #1: THE STATE

All states and governments in capitalist societies have one primary inescapable objective: they must foster and promote economic growth and capital accumulation. They have to do this because any capitalist state that ignores the necessity of assisting in the process of capital accumulation risks drying up the source of its own power and legitimacy, society's surplus production capacity, and the taxes drawn from this surplus that fund the state (O'Connor 1971). Indeed, a capitalist economy in which growth and accumulation fail to occur is one in which jobs disappear, unemployment rises, tax revenues decline, trade and budgetary deficits increase, and fiscal crises of the state abound. As these economic problems are diagnosed as political problems, the state and government's social legitimacy dissolves along with the economic structures from which its power is derived. Put simply, as industrial capitalism and the modern state have co-evolved together over the past two centuries, the state has effectively emerged as a set of institutions aimed at creating and managing the conditions under which relatively smooth growth and accumulation can occur.

As capitalist states cannot long govern societies in which growth fails to occur, they have historically carved out a central role in trying to ensure economic stability through the exercise of political power. This dynamic transcends political ideologies and economic strategies. At a general level, this historical role presupposes a vast array of specific duties including, among many others, facilitative fiscal and monetary policies, infrastructural development, coherent industrial and trade strategies, conducive social and labour policies, the creation of a legal apparatus capable of protecting private property rights, and, perhaps most significantly for our purposes here, protecting existing domestic industries and helping to seed new ones.

Strategies of accumulation

It is thus no coincidence that when we look at which countries have succeeded at climate policy, the leaders are those that have been able use climate policies as a means to enhance capital accumulation and economic growth. As Lachapelle et al. (2017) argue, the ability of states to develop strong climate policies is shaped, in large part, by their place in the global economy, and hinges on whether they have the capacity to develop an overall economic strategy that allows them to promote growth and accumulation through the innovation, production, and/or installation of low carbon technologies.

For example, a small, developing nation with high levels of indebtedness, low income levels, and a heavy dependence on high-emitting industries that produce cheap manufactured exports is not well positioned to implement a strong climate policy. To do so would likely involve stunting domestic growth and choking off the state's material resources. On the other hand, a rich country with high incomes, a diverse economy, and a strong tradition of innovation and high-tech industry is in a good position to promote greater economic growth and capital accumulation from policies that push society in toward a low-carbon future (Christoff and Eckersley 2011). So where does the Canadian economy fall along this spectrum and how does the federal government conceptualize its interests in this context?

Ottawa's interests & climate policy

When we think about how Ottawa conceptualizes its interests around climate policy, it is not as easy as simply saying that "Canada has lots of oil, and therefore we can expect that Canada will be bad at climate policy." That statement is not so much wrong as it is vastly incomplete. The way that a state or government conceptualizes its interests is actually very complex and it can pull the government of the day in many competing directions. Canada is indeed a state that relies heavily on extractive industries, and thus there has been a structural tendency for the federal government to think of growth in terms of promoting fossil fuels. But Canada also has an influential manufacturing sector that (as we will see below) is often harmed by the prominence of oil and other extractive industries. Canada has, moreover, long aspired to have a thriving R&D culture and high-tech sector that could profit enormously from renewable technologies. Added to this, the country has a prominent environmental movement that places a great deal of pressure on the state and federal government to pursue alternative growth strategies. And, finally, as we saw in Chapter 3, Canada is a federalist state whose numerous different regions have specific (and often competing) growth strategies of their own. Given that an enduring interest of all governments in Ottawa (regardless of ideology or party) is not only to promote growth, but also ensure the survival of the Canadian state and federation, Ottawa has been extremely reticent in all situations to interfere with these regional economic strategies.

In short, trying to accurately describe the interests of the Canadian state and federal government is a complicated endeavour. The state is not a homogenous entity with one single interest. Rather, states are heterogeneous bodies, and they are under constant pressure to enact policies that move the economy in different and competing directions. That said, there are a few basic indicators that give a sense of the challenges Ottawa faces in trying to reorient the economy toward a low-carbon future, without choking off the economic growth (and thus tax revenues, employment, rising standards of living, and legitimacy) that the state and government require in order to survive.

Importance of exports in an economy

There are few things more important to the strength of a domestic economy than exports. Every dollar of revenue earned from exports represents a source of new wealth that a society can use to fuel its economic growth, and, in turn, create new jobs and new sources of tax revenue, and increase its overall prosperity. A strong and growing export sector means higher foreign exchange for the host economy, which, in turn means higher purchasing power in the global market, allowing the economy to purchase more imports as the economy grows. Export growth also fuels the economy's service sector (which, in an advanced economy generally represents more than 70 percent of employment) because it creates a bigger domestic pool of wealth to invest in internal services (hospitals, schools, restaurants, the financial sector, etc.). This, in turn, means more new businesses, more jobs, higher wages, higher living standards, etc. Put simply, if a society has a strong export sector (especially one that is growing faster than overall imports), it has great potential to become wealthy and prosperous. The state and sitting government can, in turn, reap the benefits of increased material power and legitimacy.

By contrast, if export sectors are weak or declining, the economy will be adversely impacted. Lower exports will mean lower foreign exchange, which, in turn, means smaller purchasing power for imports in the global market. But it also means a reduction in the overall level of new wealth coming into the economy, which leads to a shrinking pool of wealth to invest in the service economy. This means fewer new businesses, fewer jobs, less tax revenue for the state, and less material power and legitimacy for the government. This point about exports is particularly consequential when thinking about a country's climate policies because, if a large portion of its wealth is derived from export sectors that are particularly GHG-intensive, then that country is considerably less likely to adopt policies that constrain those sectors.

Where does Canada's wealth come from? (What are its major exports?)

As depicted in Table 4.1, Canada's main exports are a mix of extractive resources and manufactured goods — many of which are particularly high-emitting. This is a big part of the reason why the energy intensity of the Canadian economy (at roughly 14 MJ per US dollar) is substantially greater than that of the US (at 9.3 MJ/$), and approximately twice that of many Western European economies.

Indeed, a look at Figure 4.1 shows that Canada's oil and gas sector, "Emissions Intensive, Trade Exposed" (EITE) industries, and agriculture industry comprised the lion's share of the country's GHG emissions in 2016. This is a problem because, in addition to serving as the lifeblood of the Canadian economy, these sectors (especially oil, gas, and agriculture) are not easy to decarbonize, as cost-effective clean technologies are not currently delivering large carbon dividends in areas like agriculture,

TABLE 4.1 TOP CANADIAN EXPORTS, 2018

SECTOR	PERCENTAGE OF TOTAL EXPORT WEALTH
Fossil fuels	20%
Cars	15%
Machinery	8%
Gems, precious metals	5%
Forestry	4%
Electronics	3%
Plastics	3%
Oil seeds	2%
Fertilizers	2%
Aluminum	2%

Source: WTEX 2018

FIGURE 4.1 CANADA'S GHG EMISSIONS BY SECTOR (CO_2E)

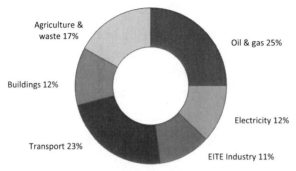

Agriculture & waste 17%

Oil & gas 25%

Buildings 12%

Electricity 12%

Transport 23%

EITE Industry 11%

Source: adapted from Government of Canada 2016b

forestry, mining, or land-use (and, obviously, the notion of decarbonizing the oil and gas sector is absurd). In this context, many elements of climate regulation are interpreted as an existential threat to these crucial sectors.

This problem is further compounded by the fact that, relative to its peer countries, Canada's economy is particularly exposed to international trade, with the sum of its imports and exports equivalent to roughly 70 percent of GDP — in most of Canada's industrialized peer countries this number tends to be around 50 percent, while in the US it is roughly 30 percent (Rivers 2009). Given Canada's exposure to trade and the energy intensity of its economy, it is not an exaggeration to suggest that stringent GHG caps (without similar actions in other countries) could have a particularly adverse impact on the national economy *as it currently exists*, likely leading to a loss of competitiveness and the associated reductions in new wealth and economic prosperity noted above.

In short, the economic sectors that would need to make the sharpest GHG cuts are those on which the economy and the federal government are most reliant. As noted above, it is these sectors that generate the greatest volume of new wealth for the country, which in turn fuels new domestic investment, job growth, increased employment, and greater revenues for the state. With that revenue, the state can provide greater services for its people, and promote the legitimacy that sitting governments require in order to survive. It is perhaps unsurprising, then, that governments in Ottawa have been so reticent to impose strict GHG regulations on a national economy that is so reliant on these industries.

How Did It Get This Way? A *Very* Brief History of the Canadian Economy

The early history of the Canadian economy was almost exclusively one of resource-led development, where raw materials were aggressively extracted and exported to core economies like the US, UK, and Europe. During this period, governments generally chose not to attempt to foster a broad diversification of the economy, or otherwise use the country's immense resource wealth to support the growth of domestic manufacturing, value-added industries, or home-grown innovation.

This all changed after the Second World War. During this time, thanks in large part to effective national and provincial industrial strategies, Canada developed a strong manufacturing sector (led by the rapid growth of the automotive, telecommunications, and aerospace sectors), and moved up the value chain with its resource sector by building value-added industries around aluminum, pulp, paper, and many others. As Stanford (2008) notes, domestic manufacturing investment was stimulated by an array of factors during this period, including the signing of the Canada–US Auto Pact, the competitive effects of Canada's public healthcare system (vis-à-vis the United States' tradition of employer-covered private insurance), the strong productivity and technological capacity of Canadian manufacturing plants, and an undervalued exchange rate against the US dollar.

From the 1970s through the 1990s, the Canadian manufacturing sector continuously outperformed those of peer countries, with manufacturing representing a larger portion of the national economy (in terms of employment and productivity) than in most other developed countries. Parallel to these developments, the relative value of foreign direct investment (FDI) into the Canadian economy began to decline dramatically, at the same time that Canadian corporations began to expand their own FDI in other countries and establish a strong presence for Canadian capital in foreign markets. In light of these successes, by the mid-1990s, unprocessed resources had, for the first time in Canadian history, come to represent less than half of the total value of Canadian exports (Stanford 2012).

In spite of this significant progress towards diversification, the past quarter-century has witnessed a structural shift back towards Canada's traditional reliance on resource-led growth, with the country's economic trajectory once again being dominated by the extraction and export of unprocessed resources. As this regression has unfolded, the Canadian economy has regained many of the characteristics that defined it throughout its early history, including a disproportionate reliance on natural resource extraction, a lack of diversification and innovation, and a heightened dependence on powerful countries for FDI (Haley 2011). Driven primarily by increased demand (and thus higher global prices) for resource inputs from China, India, and Latin America, among other regions, the past couple of decades have seen immense growth in a range of resource sectors, including potash, uranium, natural gas, agricultural and forestry products, and a range of metals and minerals (Natural Resources Canada 2012). By 2014, the aggregate value of these sectors, according to the federal government, had reached 20 percent of Canada's nominal GDP (MacNeil 2014b).

The largest and most consequential growth by far has been in the production and export of bitumen from the Alberta tar sands. As world oil prices steadily increased throughout the 2000s, unconventional methods of producing oil became gradually more cost-effective and came to represent attractive sites of investment. As a result, between 2000 and 2010, more than $117 billion worth of investment flowed into Alberta's tar sands, allowing production to more than double during that period to 1.5 million barrels per day — making Canada the fifth largest exporter of energy in the world, and raising the value of Canada's oil and gas sector to 6.7 percent of GDP (National Energy Board 2012).

The other half of this structural regression has been the decline of Canada's manufacturing and value-added industries, both of which were crucial in diversifying the economy and reducing the relative importance of resource exports in the latter half of the twentieth century. The speed and extent of this decline owes much to the rising value of the Canadian dollar in the wake of the tar sands boom, which dramatically reduced the competitiveness of manufacturing exports (Woynillowicz and Lemphers 2012). Indeed, between 2002 and 2008, the value of the Canadian dollar increased by more than 60 percent against the US dollar, causing many foreign buyers to search for cheaper sources (Stanford 2008). This played a key role in the loss of more than half a million manufacturing jobs in the early 2000s, and reducing the sector's share of national employment to its lowest point in post-war history. Of course, this decline in manufacturing, in turn, caused a dramatic increase in the relative importance of resource exports. As Stanford (2008) notes, from a low of 40 percent in 2000, the proportion of exports consisting of unprocessed resources had increased to nearly 60 percent by the end of the decade. Further buttressing this poor diversification has been a return to paltry levels of investment in innovation over the past two decades. Canadian innovation investment now ranks among the worst in the industrialized world, declining by almost one-third since 2002, where it now stands at just 0.9 percent of GDP (Conference Board of Canada 2016).

Provincial Governments' Interests

Provincial governments, much like their federal counterparts, have one consistent and enduring interest: the continuity and enhancement of economic growth. As noted above, a provincial economy that stops growing is destined for crisis. If growth cannot be achieved, domestic corporate profits will fall, unemployment will rise, tax revenues will decline, and the provincial government (unable to provide its citizens with adequate prosperity and services) will lose its legitimacy and power. How each of Canada's provincial and territorial governments goes about securing this growth not only varies quite widely in light of their historically different local economies, but it has major implications for Canadian climate policy. While it is difficult to say precisely how each government perceives its interests with regard to climate policy, a few key questions can help us to arrive at a general understanding.

The first question is simply, is the province a big polluter? Or, put differently, is the goal of rapid decarbonization a relatively straightforward

FIGURE 4.2 PER CAPITA PROVINCIAL EMISSIONS IN INTERNATIONAL CONTEXT

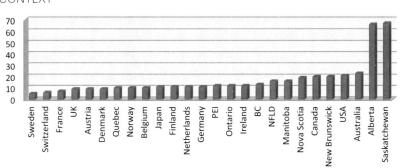

Source: adapted from Conference Board of Canada 2017

proposition, or is it something of a pipe dream? Among the ten provinces and three territories, the answer to this question varies widely, from provinces like Alberta, which emitted 68 tonnes of CO_2e per capita in 2016 (placing it on par with countries like Saudi Arabia with the highest per capita emissions on the planet), to provinces like Québec, which emitted only 10 tonnes per capita (placing it among the top tier of developed countries) (see Figures 4.2, 4.3, and 4.4). This is a crucial question for national climate policy, because any effort to decarbonize the national economy could have disproportionate impacts on certain provinces, and those jurisdictions can be expected to fight back with great fervor.

A second crucial question is, what are the province's main energy sources? Given that stationary power generation tends to be among the largest sources of emissions and the first key task of decarbonization, the nature of a province's electricity grid can be a strong determinant of its capacity and motivation to act. Here, again, we see a wide variance among the provinces, ranging from Québec and Manitoba, which have nearly emissions-free electricity grids thanks to their abundant stocks

FIGURE 4.3 PER CAPITA PROVINCIAL EMISSIONS COMPARED

Source: adapted from Environment and Climate Change Canada 2017

FIGURE 4.4 NET PROVINCIAL EMISSIONS COMPARED

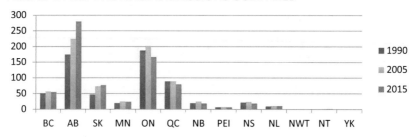

Source: adapted from Environment and Climate Change Canada 2017

of hydroelectric power, to Alberta and Saskatchewan, which get a large share of their power from coal.

A final key question is, what are the province's major exports, and to what extent are these export industries responsible for its GHG emissions? As noted above, this question gets to the very heart of how each province creates the wealth that fuels its economy, creates the new businesses which employ its citizens and create higher standards of living, and generates the tax revenues which provide the material resources to fund the government. As we will see, Canada's provinces and regions vary widely on this question, from Ontario and Québec with their highly diversified and heterogeneous economies that excel at innovation, advanced manufacturing, and IT, to many of the Prairie and Atlantic economies which rely very heavily on extractive industries. If a provincial government perceives that aggressive GHG reductions are likely to cripple its capacity to create new wealth, climate policy may be strongly resisted.

British Columbia

1. Is BC a big polluter?
With a per capita emissions rate of 13 tonnes of CO_2e, BC is one of the better performers in Canada, though not especially impressive by global standards. As noted in Figures 4.3 and 4.4, while the province's net emissions rose steadily from 1990–2005, they have since peaked, and have begun declining in both net and per capita terms.

2. What are BC's main energy sources?
With the exception of natural gas (which makes up roughly 7 percent of the province's stationary power), BC has a remarkably low-emitting power grid — owing mostly to the historical development of the province's bountiful hydroelectricity resources (see Figure 4.5). In this context, BC has a significant advantage in the process of decarbonization, and has considerable room to further reduce emissions by promoting fuel switching in the transportation sector (through electrification of vehicles) and homes/buildings (by phasing out natural gas).

FIGURE 4.5 BC POWER GRID BY SOURCE

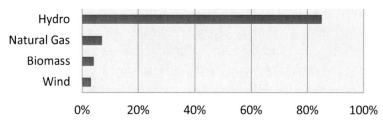

Source: adapted from National Energy Board 2017

3. Where does BC's wealth come from?

While BC is easily the most diversified economy in Western Canada, it is still very much a resource-based economy, with more than 60 percent of the value of its exports located in the resource sector. In 2016, the province's biggest export industries were coal, lumber, and wood pulp, which accounted for roughly 40 percent of the province's export revenue (see Table 4.2).

TABLE 4.2 BC'S LARGEST EXPORTS, 2016

SECTOR	PERCENTAGE OF TOTAL EXPORT WEALTH
Forestry	34%
Energy	22%
Manufacturing	14%
Minerals	13%
Agriculture	7%
Chemicals	3%
Fish/seafood	3%

Source: Government of Canada 2016a

4. To what extent are these sectors responsible for BC's GHG emissions?

Unfortunately, these industries do account for a sizeable share of BC's emissions, and thus, as a general rule, governments are likely to be reticent about policies that negatively impact them. As noted in Figure 4.6, the fossil fuel industry alone makes up nearly one-fifth of emissions, while logging, agriculture, and other heavy industry account for a considerable

FIGURE 4.6 BC'S GHG EMISSIONS BY SECTOR (CO$_2$E)

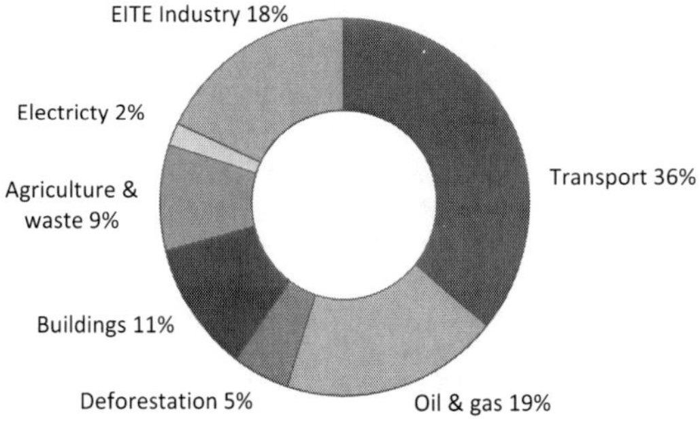

- EITE Industry 18%
- Electricty 2%
- Agriculture & waste 9%
- Buildings 11%
- Deforestation 5%
- Transport 36%
- Oil & gas 19%

Source: adapted from Government of Canada 2016b

portion as well. Moreover, these sectors are not particularly easy to decarbonize at the moment, as cost-effective clean technologies are not currently delivering large carbon dividends in areas like agriculture, forestry, or mining.

5. *How has this impacted BC's approach to climate policy?*

The BC government's approach to climate policy since the late 1980s is reflective of both the weight of its resource sector and the strength of its environmental movement. In terms of the former, while the resource sector is not nearly as influential as it is in Alberta and some other provinces, stringent regulations are still seen as constraining the development of these industries, and, with them, BC's broader economy. It is in this context that the BC government throughout the 1990s and early 2000s (despite being governed by the left-leaning NDP for much of this period) was reticent to act on climate, and, indeed, did not support Ottawa's ratification of Kyoto.

The rise of an active and ambitious provincial climate policy under Gordon Campbell's Liberal government in 2007 was largely a result of growing pressure from environmentalists to take action. But the type of action it took was also reflective of the importance of the province's resource sector. Indeed, BC's carbon tax excluded industrial process emissions — including those created by the oil and gas sector. This decision was crucial in allowing the Campbell government to gain consent from the business community.

While BC is indeed a prominent climate leader in Canada, there is still enormous potential for greater action. Given its rapidly diversifying

economy and growing high-tech sector, the province could be well positioned to find new sources of economic growth in a clean energy sector
— which, globally, is expected to be worth over $1 trillion by 2030.

Alberta

1. Is Alberta a big polluter?

At 68 tonnes of CO_2e per capita, Alberta is easily among the worst carbon polluters on the whole planet. While *per capita* emissions began to
decline after the year 2000 (thanks, at least in part, to efficiency measures
mandated by the provincial government), Alberta's net emissions continue
to grow faster than any other province's (see Figures 4.3 and 4.4). In this
context alone, by almost any metric, the task of decarbonization is, at
present, an enormously lofty goal for Alberta.

2. What are Alberta's main energy sources?

Alberta has the dirtiest power grid in the country, and one of the dirtiest in
the developed world (see Figure 4.7). Lacking the abundant hydroelectric
resources of many of its provincial brethren, the province has historically
relied on coal and natural gas to provide the bulk of its stationary power,
which respectively comprise 51 percent and 39 percent of Alberta's grid.
While this undeniably puts Alberta at an initial disadvantage in the quest
to decarbonize itself, it also means that the province has the potential to
make some dramatic early gains. Relative to other GHG emitting activities,
stationary power is considerably easier to address (sometimes referred
to as the low hanging fruit of decarbonization) in light of the rapidly
declining costs (and rapidly increasing efficiencies) of renewable and

FIGURE 4.7 ALBERTA POWER GRID BY SOURCE

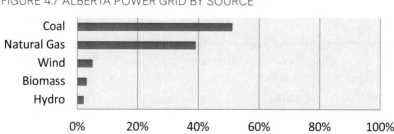

Source: adapted from National Energy Board 2017

storage technologies, particularly wind and solar. Indeed, Alberta and Saskatchewan have the greatest solar energy potential of all the provinces and territories. If Alberta were to make serious investments in these technologies, it could not only reduce emissions from its grid, but also begin to address issues like transportation through electrification of its vehicle fleet.

3. Where does Alberta's wealth come from?

As one would expect, the *vast* majority of Alberta's wealth comes from oil and gas. In 2016, the sector accounted for more than 70 percent of the province's export value (see Table 4.3).

TABLE 4.3 ALBERTA'S LARGEST EXPORTS, 2016

SECTOR	PERCENTAGE OF TOTAL EXPORT WEALTH
Fossil fuels	72%
Agriculture	9%
Chemicals & plastics	8%
Manufacturing	6%
Forestry	2%

Source: Government of Canada 2016a

It is difficult to overstate the role that oil has played in growing Alberta's economy since the 1960s, both raising the living standards of its residents and providing material power and social legitimacy to the government. As a result of oil exports, Alberta's per capita and net GDP has grown faster than any other Canadian province or US state (and, indeed, faster than just about any other developed economy in the world), providing Albertans with average incomes that were 61 percent higher than the Canadian average in 2012. While the oil industry directly provides less than 8 percent of overall employment in the province, its spin-off effects have generated growth across the whole economy, helping to create over a half million new jobs between 2004 and 2014. By the same token, however, when the global price of oil crashed after 2014, the Albertan economy shed over 100,000 jobs.

4. To what extent are these sectors responsible for Alberta's emissions?

Unfortunately (and unsurprisingly) Alberta's oil and gas sector accounts for the lion's share of the province's GHG emissions, and thus governments have typically been extremely hostile to any policies aimed at reigning them in. Between the consumption of fossil fuels during the extraction process and the large amounts of fugitive emissions from mining, the sector accounted for roughly half of Alberta's carbon pollution in 2016. Making matters worse, forestry, agriculture, and emissions-intensive manufacturing make up a further one-fifth of the province's overall export wealth, and, as Figure 4.8 depicts, are also responsible for a healthy share of overall emissions. At the moment, cost effective clean technologies are not widely available for decarbonizing these sectors (and, it goes without saying, one cannot decarbonize the oil and gas sector), and thus climate policy confronts these industries as something of a non-negotiable existential threat.

FIGURE 4.8 ALBERTA'S GHG EMISSIONS BY SECTOR (CO_2E)

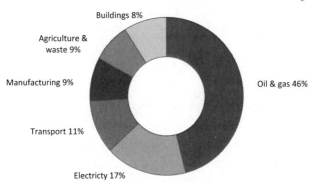

Source: adapted from Government of Canada 2016b

5. How has this impacted Alberta's approach to climate policy?

In light of the above, it should come as no surprise that Alberta has long been the province most aggressively opposed to national climate regulation. Despite continued rhetoric over the past few decades about the need to drastically diversify the provincial economy, the basic enduring interest of all Alberta governments for the past fifty years has been to ensure that the oil and gas keeps flowing. In addition to its role in propping up all other major employment sectors in the province, the industry is typically responsible for nearly half of all government revenue (Carter 2007), meaning that the government has an enormous structural reliance on it. The extremely close ties between the industry and Progressive Conservative Party (now the United Conservative Party) have exacerbated this reliance, with the oil and gas lobby donating millions to Conservative politicians during the Party's forty-four year hold on power from 1971 through 2015.

In addition to a below-average environmental consciousness in the province, Carter (2007) notes that the vast majority of Albertans believe that they benefit immensely from oil sands development and thus are extremely reluctant to challenge it. As the author suggests, oil-based affluence in Alberta has created an astonishing level of political complacency. "Much is tolerated or ignored in exchange for the semblance of oil wealth" (2007: 14). As if to underscore this point, in 2005, Premier Ralph Klein began a policy of distributing so-called prosperity bonuses of $400 to all Alberta residents, to reward their hard work and distribute his government's massive oil-fuelled surplus budgets. Moreover, to the extent that environmental opposition does exist, it has rarely found any substantive expression in light of the province's "democratic deficit," which, as noted above, featured single-party rule from 1971 through 2015, exceptionally low voter turnout, and general elections that, according to Dabbs (2006), were merely ceremonial in nature.

As a result, since the early 1990s, the Alberta government has had a strong interest in preventing the passage of federal climate policy, and has thus engaged in the national policy process more aggressively and disruptively than any other province. As noted in Chapter 2, not only did Alberta consistently play spoiler in the consensus-based NAPCC process, but it actually took the unexpected step of being the first province to implement its own climate policy, largely as a symbolic act to ward off any further federal pressure.

Saskatchewan

1. Is Saskatchewan a big polluter?
At the time of writing, Saskatchewan holds the title for being the worst *per capita* carbon polluter in Canada. Indeed, at 71 tonnes of CO_2e per resident in 2015, there are few other economies in the world that can compete with

Saskatchewan on this measure. While the province's per capita emissions have declined slightly since the late 2000s, its net emissions have continued to grow at an alarming rate (see Figures 4.3 and 4.4). In fact, in terms of net emissions, Saskatchewan was roughly on par with Québec in 2015, despite the fact that Québec's population is over eight times the size of Saskatchewan's.

2. What are Saskatchewan's main energy sources?

Much like its neighbour Alberta, Saskatchewan has an energy grid that has historically relied heavily on fossil fuels (see Figure 4.9). As of 2015, Saskatchewan was producing over 80 percent of its stationary power from a combination of coal and natural gas, thus providing the province with one of the dirtiest power grids in the country. As noted in the case of Alberta, while this places Saskatchewan at an early disadvantage, it also provides an opportunity to make reasonably easy gains by investing in renewables and storage technologies — particularly as Saskatchewan has the greatest solar energy potential of any province in Canada.

FIGURE 4.9 SASKATCHEWAN POWER GRID BY SOURCE

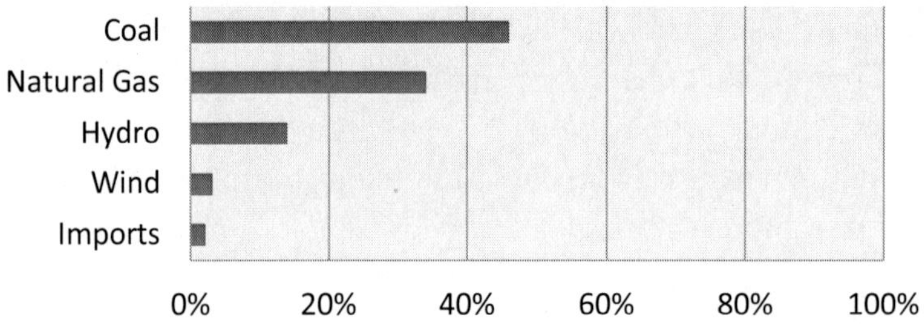

Source: adapted from National Energy Board 2017

3. Where does Saskatchewan's wealth come from?

Saskatchewan's economy has grown quite wealthy over the past few decades on the back of its resource exports, with primary industries accounting for well over 80 percent of the province's export value in 2016. Indeed, Saskatchewan has become a prominent exporter of oil, coal, potash, uranium, wheat, fertilizer, meat products, mineral fuels, and pulp and paper — earning the province the moniker of "Canada's bread basket." With these exports equivalent to over 70 percent of the province's GDP, it is fair to say that, in the absence of such an impressive resource sector, Saskatchewan would have one of the smaller and poorer economies in Canada (see Table 4.4).

TABLE 4.4 SASKATCHEWAN'S LARGEST EXPORTS, 2016

SECTOR	PERCENTAGE OF TOTAL EXPORT WEALTH
Agriculture	49%
Oil	19%
Potash	18%
Uranium	4%

Source: Government of Canada 2016a

4. To what extent are these sectors responsible for Saskatchewan's emissions?

Regrettably, as depicted in Figure 4.10, an enormous share of Saskatchewan's GHG emissions derive from these crucial industries, making governments highly resistant to climate policies that would threaten them. Indeed, nearly half of the province's entire emissions profile came from the oil and gas, mining, and agriculture sectors in 2016 — none of which have access to cost effective clean technologies that could help to easily decarbonize them. By any metric, addressing GHG emissions in Saskatchewan would have major implications for the province's current sources of wealth.

FIGURE 4.10 SASKATCHEWAN'S GHG EMISSIONS BY SECTOR (CO_2E)

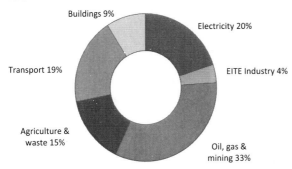

Source: adapted from Government of Canada 2016b

5. How has this impacted Saskatchewan's approach to climate policy?

Given the province's massive reliance on these heavy-emitting sectors for its wealth, employment, and prosperity, the Saskatchewan government has, unsurprisingly, been extremely reticent to take any aggressive action on climate. Even while governed by the left-leaning NDP throughout the 1990s and early 2000s, Saskatchewan adopted a reactionary stance, with Premier Roy Romanow's government shutting down the province's Energy Conservation and Development Commission and passing a resolution in the legislature denouncing the Kyoto Protocol, insisting that no federal regulations be placed on the provinces. When a modest environmental opposition did arise in the early 2000s in the form of the New Green Alliance, NDP Premier Lorne Calvert eventually introduced a set of goals for GHG emissions reductions, but never made a serious attempt to actually achieve them. Even during the negotiation of a new national climate framework under the Trudeau government in 2016, Saskatchewan proved to be the most aggressively opposed province, with Premier Brad Wall leading the legal effort to prevent Ottawa from imposing a carbon price.

Manitoba

1. Is Manitoba a big polluter?

At 16 tonnes of CO_2e per capita, Manitoba would be considered a mid-level GHG polluter in the Canadian context — though by the standard of other developed economies around the world, it would be considered a major polluter. That said, however, since the early 2000s, the province has seen its emissions slowly begin to decline in both net and per capita terms (see Figures 4.3 and 4.4).

2. What are Manitoba's main energy sources?

Manitoba has been blessed with enormous hydroelectric resources, which have been used to build one of the lowest-emitting power grids in the world (see Figure 4.11). With a little over 97 percent of the province's stationary power provided by hydro in 2015, Manitoba has an enviable starting point for the process of decarbonization.

FIGURE 4.11 MANITOBA POWER GRID BY SOURCE

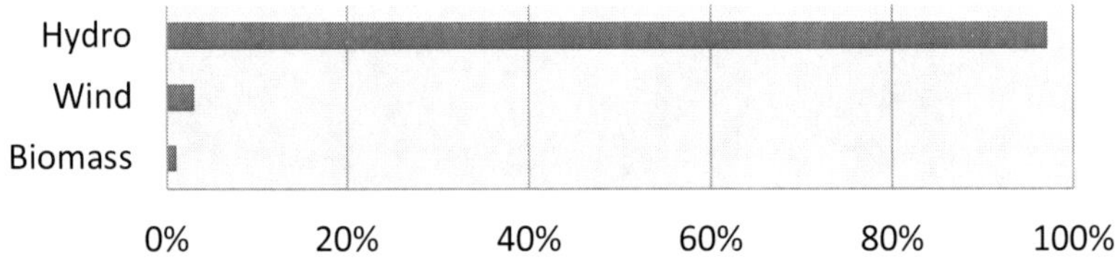

Source: adapted from National Energy Board 2017

3. Where does Manitoba's wealth come from?

Manitoba's economy is considerably more diversified than its Prairie neighbours, with roughly 70 percent of the value of its exports coming from manufacturing and value-added industries in 2016. The other approximately 30 percent came from resource industries, in particular agriculture, oil, forestry, and mining. The southern and western parts of the province are home to more than 10 percent of Canada's arable farmland, where more than a third of all farming activity is the GHG-intensive process of cattle raising (see Table 4.5).

TABLE 4.5 MANITOBA'S LARGEST EXPORTS, 2016

SECTOR	PERCENTAGE OF TOTAL EXPORT WEALTH
Manufacturing	65%
Agriculture	22%
Mining	7%
Energy	3%

Source: Government of Canada 2016a

4. To what extent are these sectors responsible for Manitoba's GHG emissions?

As depicted in Figure 4.12, Manitoba's biggest challenge is its agriculture sector, which creates significant GHG emissions in the form of methane from livestock and nitrous oxide from soils. And, as noted, at the moment, there is not a wide array of cost-effective clean technologies that could help to fix this problem. Beyond that, however, the rest of Manitoba's emissions profile is relatively unrelated to its major wealth-generating sectors. Investments in technology and efficiency improvements in its manufacturing sector could go a long way toward helping decarbonize this branch of the economy.

FIGURE 4.12 MANITOBA'S GHG EMISSIONS BY SECTOR (CO_2E)

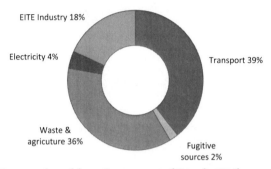

EITE Industry 18%

Electricity 4%

Transport 39%

Waste &
agriculture 36%

Fugitive
sources 2%

Source: adapted from Government of Canada 2016b

5. How has this impacted Manitoba's approach to climate policy?

In light of these advantages, Manitoba was, for many years, one of the strongest supporters of climate policy in the country. In fact, along with Québec, it was one of only two provinces to support the federal government's ratification of Kyoto in the early 2000s.

In 2008, driven by Ottawa's failure to act, NDP Premier Gary Doer made Manitoba the first jurisdiction in North America to pass legislation committing the province to firm GHG reduction targets. He also partnered with subnational leaders in the US to form both the Western Climate Initiative (WCI) and the Midwestern Greenhouse Gas Reduction Accord (MGGRA), and committed Manitoba to a cap-and-trade program and tough new standards to reduce emissions from vehicles and fuels. As a province with a small population and enormous hydroelectric resources, Manitoba indeed appeared well positioned to derive new sources of wealth through an active climate policy — particularly given its capacity to sell carbon-free energy to a series of neighbouring US states that were committing to substantial emissions cuts under these regional climate accords (B. Boyd 2015).

With the onset of the global financial crisis, however, Manitoba's climate ambitions largely fell apart. By late 2009, it had become clear that the US was not going to implement a national cap-and-trade program or Renewable Portfolio Standard, nor were any members of the WCI or MGGRA in a position to fulfill their pledges under the respective accords. Indeed, by the end of 2010, the MGGRA had been abandoned, and six states had withdrawn from the WCI. At the same time, Manitoba's agriculture, forestry, mining, and oil and gas industries began to put significant pressure on the government to abandon its climate targets in light of the deteriorating economy. In the ensuing years, the NDP government abandoned most of its climate initiatives, deciding that the economic risks outweighed the potential opportunities. With the election of a PC majority government in 2016, Manitoba quickly became one of the least cooperative provinces on national climate policy, joining Saskatchewan in opposing the Trudeau government's efforts to impose a carbon price on obstinate provinces.

Ontario

1. Is Ontario a big polluter?

Relative to other Canadian provinces and most developed economies around the world, Ontario is a reasonably modest carbon polluter. While its net emissions are surpassed only by Alberta, this owes largely to the fact that it is home to nearly 40 percent of Canada's population. Moreover, in terms of per capita emissions, Ontario has the third lowest, at 12 tonnes of CO_2e. In both net and per capita terms, the province's emissions have been declining since the mid 2000s (see Figures 4.3 and 4.4).

2. What are Ontario's main energy sources?

Thanks to sizeable government investments in nuclear and hydroelectric power throughout the post-war period — and more recent investments in wind and solar — Ontario has a remarkably low-emitting power grid, deriving less than 7 percent of its stationary power from fossil fuels (see Figure 4.13).

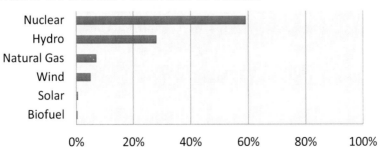

FIGURE 4.13 ONTARIO POWER GRID BY SOURCE

Source: adapted from National Energy Board 2017

3. Where does Ontario's wealth come from?

Ontario has one of the more diversified economies in Canada, accounting for nearly half of the country's manufacturing GDP in 2016. As depicted in Table 4.6, Ontario's economy is heavily reliant on automobile manufacturing, but also has a large resource sector as well.

TABLE 4.6 ONTARIO'S LARGEST EXPORTS, 2016

SECTOR	PERCENTAGE OF TOTAL EXPORT WEALTH
Cars	37%
Precious metals	16%
Machinery	12%
Electronics	8%
Plastics	6%
Iron/steel	6%
Nickel	5%
Forestry	5%
Agriculture	5%

Source: Government of Canada 2016a

4. To what extent are these sectors responsible for Ontario's GHG emissions?

As noted in Figure 4.14, one of Ontario's biggest emissions sources is indeed its large industrial manufacturing sector, which was responsible for nearly one-third of the province's emissions in 2015. However, decarbonization is not necessarily an existential threat to this sector, as relatively straightforward investments in technology and efficiency improvements could go a long way toward reducing its emissions. With the exception of its agricultural sector, Ontario's overall emissions profile is considerably less related to its major wealth-generating sectors than many other province's. Its biggest challenge by far is transport. While the province's overall emissions have declined over the past several years, emissions from transport continue to rise and currently sit at 27 percent above 1990s levels. This, however, could be addressed relatively easily by using Ontario's low-carbon electricity grid to power the electrification of the province's vehicle fleet.

FIGURE 4.14 ONTARIO'S GHG EMISSIONS BY SECTOR (CO$_2$E)

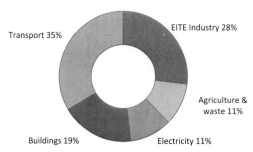

Transport 35%

EITE Industry 28%

Agriculture & waste 11%

Buildings 19%

Electricity 11%

Source: adapted from Government of Canada 2016b

5. How has this impacted Ontario's approach to climate policy?

Given its industrial diversification, Ontario simultaneously has numerous industries that are threatened by aggressive climate policies, and numerous that could stand to benefit. For this reason, while most provinces show a fair amount continuity on climate policy between political parties, Ontario's approach has depended almost entirely on which party is in power.

Throughout the late 1990s and early 2000s, the right-wing PC majority governments of Mike Harris chose to adopt a more pessimistic approach, viewing climate regulation as an existential threat to the province's sizeable manufacturing sector (particularly its automotive industry). Also, given its staunch neoliberal ideology, Harris' government was hostile to the forms of intervention required to, for example, reform the province's utilities by closing its coal plants. For this reason, Ontario not only opposed Kyoto, but also aligned closely with Alberta throughout the NAPCC negotiations, helping to grind the process to a halt.

In 2003, however, Dalton McGuinty's Liberals formed a majority government and soon changed Ontario's position to that of a more willing participant on climate. While their capacity to take aggressive action was still hampered by the province's car industry, McGuinty nevertheless took significant steps to eliminate all coal-fired electricity plants in Ontario, promote renewables with a province-wide feed-in tariff, and invest in greater public transport options. Later, under Liberal Premier Kathleen Wynne, the province also joined the WCI's cap-and-trade program. Coupled with broader shifts in the Ontario economy, these policies helped to generate significant emissions reductions after the mid-2000s. As of 2018, however, the election of PC Premier Doug Ford has seen a new era of hostility toward climate regulation, with Ford scrapping the lion's share of his predecessor's climate policies within months of taking office.

Québec

1. Is Québec a big polluter?

At 10 tonnes of CO_2e per capita, Québec has the lowest emissions in Canada and ranks quite respectably among developed countries across the globe. As depicted in Figures 4.3 and 4.4, Québec also stands out as the only province whose net and per capita emissions have both been declining for the better part of thirty years.

2. What are Québec's main energy sources?

As depicted in Figure 4.15, Québec's vast hydroelectric resources have allowed the province to construct a nearly carbon-free power grid, providing it with a tremendous structural advantage in the quest for decarbonization.

FIGURE 4.15 QUÉBEC POWER GRID BY SOURCE

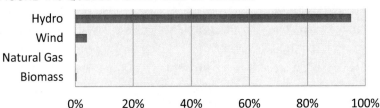

Source: adapted from National Energy Board 2017

3. Where does Québec's wealth come from?

Like its neighbour Ontario, Québec has a highly diversified economy, with manufactured and value-added goods comprising the majority of the province's export profile (see Table 4.7).

TABLE 4.7 QUÉBEC'S LARGEST EXPORTS, 2016

SECTOR	PERCENTAGE OF TOTAL EXPORT WEALTH
Aluminum	19%
Aircraft	16%
Machinery	9%
Energy	9%
Electronics	8%
Paper	7%
Copper	7%
Agriculture	7%
Forestry	6%
Plastic	6%
Precious metals	5%

Source: Government of Canada 2016a

4. To what extent are these export sectors responsible for Québec's emissions?

As depicted in Figure 4.16, one of Québec's biggest emissions sources is its large manufacturing sector, which was responsible for 32 percent of emissions in 2016. Yet climate regulation is not necessarily an existential threat to this sector, as investments in efficiency could go a long way toward reducing its emissions. With the exception of its agricultural sector, Québec's emissions profile is relatively unrelated to major

FIGURE 4.16 QUÉBEC'S GHG EMISSIONS BY SECTOR (CO$_2$E)

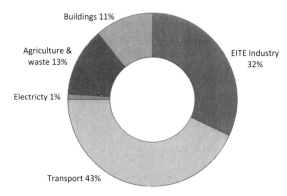

Source: adapted from Government of Canada 2016b

wealth-generating sectors. Much like Ontario, its biggest challenge by far is transportation, which could be addressed by leveraging its carbon-free power grid to electrify the province's vehicle fleet.

5. How has this impacted Québec's approach to climate policy?

Given its capacity to sell hydroelectricity to neighbouring jurisdictions, a carbon constrained North America has long presented itself as a crucial economic opportunity for Québec. In this context, the Québec government, under the control of both major parties, has been one of the stand-out leaders among Canadian provinces. Beginning in 1995, the Parti Québécois (PQ) government began participating actively in the dialogue over national climate policy, implementing its own version of the Voluntary Challenge and Registry program. Later, in 2001, it passed a resolution calling on Ottawa to ratify Kyoto — joining Manitoba as the only other province to support ratification.

One of Québec's biggest challenges in developing a serious climate strategy is its large aluminum industry — which is simultaneously one of the province's biggest export sectors *and* biggest GHG emitters. Nevertheless, under both PQ and Liberal governments, the industry entered into agreements with the province designed to achieve absolute emissions reductions (while also increasing production and profitability) through efficiency measures. As part of the deal, the province agreed to help control the costs of compliance.

As noted in Chapter 3, in 2007, Québec made further strides by implementing a small carbon tax on specific sectors. Later, in 2012, the province initiated its cap-and-trade program as part of WCI, under which the province agreed to provide free emissions allowances to any industries exposed to international competition. As Houle, Lachapelle, and Purdon (2015) note, neither the carbon tax of 2007 nor the cap-and-trade program of 2012 were ever questioned by either of the province's two major parties, indicating "a far-reaching elite consensus among the main political parties about the scientific basis of human-induced climate change and on the legitimacy of market-based instruments." Indeed, even the right-wing Coalition Avenir Québec that came to power in 2018 refused to take a hostile stance on climate. This is undoubtedly buttressed by the electorate's unparalleled support for climate action. In national surveys conducted by Mildenberger et al. (2016), Québecers were the most likely in Canada to agree with the science of anthropogenic climate change, with the numbers of those indicating a belief reaching above 90 percent in the Metro Montréal area, and only one of the province's seventy-eight federal ridings averaging below 50 percent belief. Québecers were also the most likely in Canada to support a price on carbon, with 57 percent of respondents indicating their support for a carbon tax (and rising above 75 percent in the Montréal area) and 67 percent supporting a cap-and-trade program.

New Brunswick

1. Is New Brunswick a big polluter?
New Brunswick's 20 tonnes of CO_2e per capita make it one of the biggest polluters in Canada (though obviously nowhere near the extent of its cousins in Alberta and Saskatchewan). On the positive side, however, as of 2015, the province's net and per capita emissions had both been declining for more than a decade, after having peaked in the early 2000s (see Figures 4.3 and 4.4).

2. What are New Brunswick's main energy sources?
While New Brunswick's energy matrix includes a fair amount of renewables in the form of hydro, nuclear, and wind, the province still gets most of its power from a combination of coal, natural gas, and diesel. As depicted in Figure 4.17, this is indeed the source of the lion's share of the province's GHG emissions.

FIGURE 4.17 NEW BRUNSWICK POWER GRID BY SOURCE

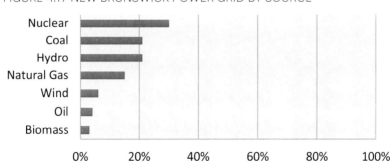

Source: adapted from National Energy Board 2017

3. Where does New Brunswick's wealth come from?

As depicted in Table 4.8, New Brunswick is a resouce economy through and through. In particular, New Brunswick's economy is heavily reliant on the export of fossil fuels, with 63 percent of the value of all exports coming from oil in 2016, while the remainder came mostly from a combination of other primary sector industries.

TABLE 4.8 NEW BRUNSWICK'S LARGEST EXPORTS, 2016

SECTOR	PERCENTAGE OF TOTAL EXPORT WEALTH
Oil	61%
Fish/seafood	11%
Paper	7%
Wood	7%
Fertilizers	5%
Agriculture	4%
Minerals & metals	3%

Source: Government of Canada 2016a

4. To what extent are these sectors responsible for New Brunswick's emissions?

Unfortunately, as might be expected, a large chunk of New Brunswick's GHG emissions come from the oil and gas sector — which, for obvious reasons, is not particularly amenable to decarbonization efforts. Besides this, however, most of the province's emissions are unrelated to its major wealth-generating sectors (see Figure 4.18).

FIGURE 4.18 NEW BRUNSWICK'S GHG EMISSIONS BY SECTOR (CO_2E)

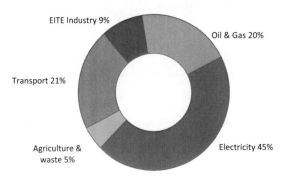

Source: adapted from Government of Canada 2016b

5. How has this impacted New Brunswick's approach to climate policy?

Given New Brunswick's heavy reliance on oil exports and its fossil fuel based power grid, most governments have interpreted stringent carbon regulations as a threat to the province and its economy. At the same time however, as an Atlantic province, the physical impacts of climate change are of great concern to New Brunswick, with the government expecting the province to incur "significant economic losses due to the impacts of extreme weather events … rising sea levels and temperature, coastal erosion, decreasing snowfalls, and flooding" (cited in Houle and Macdonald 2011). As a result, the New Brunswick government's position on climate policy over the past thirty years has been somewhat erratic, as leaders have tried to navigate the implied trade-offs between current economic stability and the province's long-term health. In the main, however, New Brunswick has not been a leader on the issue, taking a stand against Kyoto's ratification and resisting substantive federal regulatory efforts throughout the 1990s and 2000s. Indeed, at the time of writing, the province is moving forward with a strategy to aggressively expand shale-gas exploration along its coastline, promising to dramatically increase its overall emissions.

Prince Edward Island

1. Is PEI a big polluter?

With its small population of just over 140,000 residents, it likely comes as no surprise that PEI is the smallest net emitter of all the provinces. But at 12 tonnes of CO_2e per capita, it is also the second smallest per capita polluter in the country. PEI's emissions (both net and per capita) peaked in the early 2000s, and have been slowly declining ever since (see Figures 4.3 and 4.4).

2. What are PEI's main energy sources?

PEI is unique among Canadian provinces not merely for its small size, but also for the fact that it is the only jurisdiction that basically lacks a domestic supply of baseload power. For this reason, PEI imports much of its energy from New Brunswick via submarine cables installed in the late 1970s. Given the expense and vulnerability of this set up, the island has worked hard over the past several years to wean itself off imported power (which is largely generated by fossil fuels), setting aggressive renewable energy targets and aiming to construct two new wind farms capable of generate 70MW of clean power by 2025. As of 2016, 15 percent of PEI's grid was powered by wind.

3. Where does PEI's wealth come from?

While Prince Edward Island has a small manufacturing and aerospace sector, the island is the quintessential resource economy, deriving the vast majority of its export wealth from agricultural products like potatoes, frozen fruits and vegetables, and seafood (see Table 4.9).

TABLE 4.9 PEI'S LARGEST EXPORTS, 2016

SECTOR	PERCENTAGE OF TOTAL EXPORT WEALTH
Prepared potatoes/veggies	26%
Agriculture	21%
Fish/seafood	17%
Aerospace products	9%
Machinery	8%
Chemicals	7%

Source: Government of Canada 2016a

4. To what extent are these sectors responsible for PEI's emissions?

Unfortunately, given the nature of its economy, a large share of PEI's emissions derives from the agricultural sector, which is vital to the province's overall economic health. As noted above, this is not a sector whose GHG

FIGURE 4.19 PEI'S GHG EMISSIONS BY SECTOR (CO_2E)

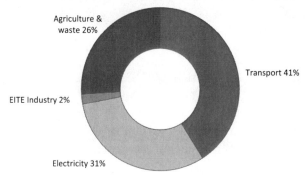

Source: adapted from Government of Canada 2016b

pollution can be easily reduced through cost effective clean technologies. Stationary power comprises nearly a third of emissions, largely in light of the island's reliance on imports from New Brunswick's fossil fuel based power grid (see Figure 4.19).

5. How has this impacted PEI's approach to climate policy?

Like its fellow Atlantic provinces, PEI faces some of the most pressing physical threats from climate change, including rising sea levels, coastal erosion, extreme weather events, and declining agricultural yields. Unlike its fellow Atlantic provinces, however, PEI has a better structural starting point for decarbonization, lacking a large industrial base and needing to design a more secure and independent energy system. As a result, while it would be generous to call PEI a climate leader like BC or Québec, the province has nonetheless been taking action for the better part of two decades, most notably through its renewable energy strategy, which has seen the construction of multiple large wind farms on the island since the early 2000s.

Nova Scotia

1. Is Nova Scotia a big polluter?

At 18 tonnes of CO_2e per capita, Nova Scotia is the fourth largest GHG polluter in Canada. While its net and per capita emissions both rose steadily throughout the 1990s and early 2000s, both have since peaked and entered into decline (see Figures 4.3 and 4.4).

2. What are Nova Scotia's main energy sources?

While Nova Scotia has made significant strides to reduce its domestic coal consumption since the early 2000s, it nevertheless still has one of the dirtier grids in Canada, generating roughly three-quarters of its electricity from a combination of coal, natural gas, and oil (see Figure 4.20).

3. Where does Nova Scotia's wealth come from?

Like its fellow Atlantic provinces, Nova Scotia is largely a resource-based economy, with the majority of its export profile composed of a mix of agricultural, forestry, and seafood products (see Table 4.10). Its economy has, nevertheless, undergone notable diversification over the past two

FIGURE 4.20 NOVA SCOTIA POWER GRID BY SOURCE

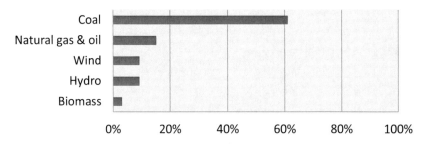

Source: adapted from National Energy Board 2017

decades following the collapse of the cod fisheries, the decline of coal mining in Cape Breton, and the closure of the province's major steel mill in the mid 1990s. As a result, industries like aerospace and offshore oil and gas production have become increasingly important to the province.

TABLE 4.10 NOVA SCOTIA'S LARGEST EXPORTS, 2016

SECTOR	PERCENTAGE OF TOTAL EXPORT WEALTH
Rubber	26%
Fish/seafood	21%
Oil/gas	17%
Forestry	15%
Aerospace products	8%
Plastics	3%

Source: Government of Canada 2016a

4. To what extent are these sectors responsible for Nova Scotia's emissions?

Aside from its oil and gas sector (which generates a sizeable portion of the province's emissions), Nova Scotia's GHG profile is actually relatively unrelated to its major wealth-generating sectors, suggesting that climate regulation is not an existential threat to the province's economy.

5. How has this impacted Nova Scotia's approach to climate policy?

Given Nova Scotia's reliance on oil exports and its fossil fuel based energy grid, its governments have generally viewed climate regulation as a threat to the province's economy. Like its fellow Atlantic provinces, however, Nova

FIGURE 4.21 NOVA SCOTIA'S GHG EMISSIONS BY SECTOR (CO_2E)

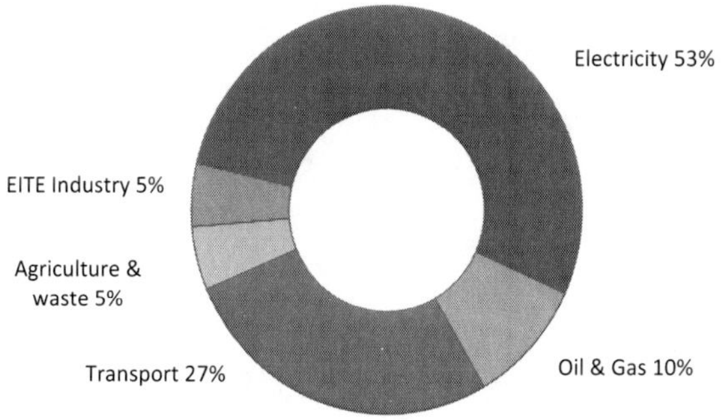

- Electricity 53%
- EITE Industry 5%
- Agriculture & waste 5%
- Transport 27%
- Oil & Gas 10%

Source: adapted from Government of Canada 2016b

Scotia is also highly vulnerable to the physical impacts of climate change. As the PC government noted in 2007, the effects of rising sea levels and extreme storms will be particularly devastating for Nova Scotia given that "most of our population lives along the coastline, and much of our infrastructure is located in vulnerable areas" (cited in Houle and Macdonald 2011). As a result, the government's position on climate policy over the past thirty years has been somewhat mixed, generally favouring incumbent industries. In particular, throughout the 1990s and 2000s, Nova Scotia was one of the more reactionary provinces on climate, having not only opposed Kyoto's ratification, but also spearheading an initiative with Alberta and Saskatchewan to condemn any federal efforts to impose climate regulations.

Newfoundland & Labrador

1. Is Newfoundland & Labrador a big polluter?

At 16 tonnes of CO_2e per capita, Newfoundland & Labrador is in the middle of the pack of Canadian provinces and would be considered a poor performer among most developed economies around the globe. While the province's net emissions have risen slightly since the early 1990s, its per capita emissions have been steadily declining since 2005 (see Figures 4.3 and 4.4).

2. What are Newfoundland & Labrador's main energy sources?

Newfoundland & Labrador has historically derived the lion's share of its grid power from hydroelectricity, which accounted for 94 percent of stationary power in 2017. The remaining 6 percent came from an even split between oil and natural gas (see Figure 4.22).

FIGURE 4.22 NL POWER GRID BY SOURCE

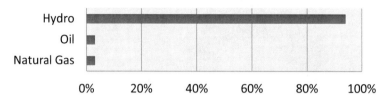

Source: adapted from National Energy Board 2017

3. Where does Newfoundland & Labrador's wealth come from?

Following the collapse of the cod fisheries in the early 1990s, Newfoundland & Labrador's economy fell into a prolonged slump, with persistently high unemployment, stagnant growth, and a noteworthy decrease in population as residents moved west in search of better opportunities. Since the early 2000s, however, the province has experienced a significant turnaround thanks to a major energy and resource boom, centred mainly on offshore oil and gas production (see Table 4.11). As a result, over the past decade, the province has experienced GDP growth well above the national average, declining unemployment rates, surplus budgets, rising wages, and a growing population.

TABLE 4.11 NL'S LARGEST EXPORTS, 2016

SECTOR	PERCENTAGE OF TOTAL EXPORT WEALTH
Oil/gas	57%
Iron ore	25%
Fish/seafood	9%
Aircraft parts	4%
Paper	3%
Meat	2%

Source: Government of Canada 2016a

4. To what extent are these sectors responsible for Newfoundland & Labrador's emissions?

Unfortunately, much like its fellow fossil fuel-producing provinces, a sizeable percentage of Newfoundland & Labrador's emissions come from its oil and gas sector (see Figure 4.23). As this sector is now a key lifeline for

FIGURE 4.23 NL'S GHG EMISSIONS BY SECTOR (CO$_2$E)

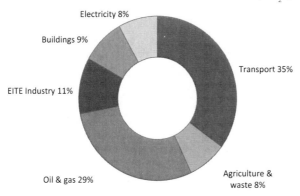

Electricity 8%

Buildings 9%

Transport 35%

EITE Industry 11%

Oil & gas 29%

Agriculture &
waste 8%

Source: adapted from Government of Canada 2016b

the province's economy (and given that this is not a sector that is amenable to decarbonization), any climate regulation designed to reign it in is likely to be viewed with hostility.

5. How has this impacted Newfoundland & Labrador's approach to climate policy?

Newfoundland & Labrador's possession of large amounts of exportable oil *and* hydroelectric power has created an unusual operating space for the province on climate policy. On the one hand, the combination of the province's hydroelectric resources and its unique vulnerability to the impacts of climate change have caused the government, at various times, to advocate for greater action on climate. Yet, given the role that fossil fuel exploration has played in buoying Newfoundland & Labrador's economy since the early 2000s, the government has tended to strongly resist any pressure to act and (under a Liberal government) scorned Chrétien's efforts to ratify Kyoto and develop federal climate regulations in the early 2000s. The PC government of the mid 2000s embodied this cognitive dissonance in a provincial climate assessment, when it noted that, while many of the anticipated impacts of climate change will be enormously detrimental to Newfoundland & Labrador, others will be positive for the oil and gas industry, which will benefit from thinner ice off the province's coast. The report concludes that the province must "develop a plan that treats ... oil and gas fairly and recognizes the contribution these industries make to the provincial economy" (cited in Houle and Macdonald 2011).

Nunavut, Yukon, & the Northwest Territories

1. Are the territories big polluters?

In terms of net emissions, Canada's three territories barely crack a tenth of 1 percent of the country's total. Yet with their small populations (just a little over 100,000) and the energy requirements of living in the high north, the territories actually have some of the highest per capita emissions in Canada. This ranges from 16 tonnes of CO_2e in the Yukon, to 18 tonnes in Nunavut, and 33 tonnes in the Northwest Territories.

2. What are the territories' main energy sources?

Across the three jurisdictions, we see a range of answers to this question. While Yukon's electricity grid is one of the most decarbonized in the country (deriving 95 percent of its power from hydro, and the remainder from oil), the same cannot be said of its eastern neighbours. While the Northwest Territories have made significant strides in installing renewables like wind and solar over the past several years, they nevertheless still derive more than three-quarters of their energy from fossil fuels (chiefly diesel and natural gas). Nunavut's energy system is the most unique in Canada for a couple reasons. First, Nunavut is the only jurisdiction that does not have a shared transmission grid. While other provinces and territories have unified grids that connect cities and communities along a shared transmission grid, Nunavut uses a series of independent microgrids to power each local area. And, related to this, Nunavut does not have any local energy sources, and thus virtually all power throughout the territory is provided by imported fossil fuels, which are used to run generators in each community.

3. Where does the territories' wealth come from?

All three territories have remarkably similar economies, with precious metals and mineral mining providing the overwhelming majority (in excess of 90 percent) of export wealth.

4. To what extent are these sectors responsible for the territories' emissions?

Unfortunately, mining activity is a significant source of carbon pollution in each jurisdiction, averaging roughly one-third of overall emissions across the territories as a whole. As with other resource-rich provinces noted above, this has created a situation where the lifeblood of the territories' economies can be perceived as threatened by climate regulation. The biggest issue for the territories, however, is transportation. Given their expansive land masses and the heightened use of air travel for mining and exports, transportation is responsible for roughly half of all carbon emissions in each territory.

5. How has this impacted the territories' approach to climate policy?

Given their collective exposure to some of the worst physical effects of climate change, the three territory governments have long been vocal supporters of federal action on the issue. However, all three have opposed federally imposed obligations upon them, arguing that Inuit communities struggling with fragile economies and high costs of living are in no position to make sacrifices, particularly given their small populations and miniscule contribution to Canada's overall emissions. Instead, the territory governments have consistently called for more federal assistance to modernize their energy infrastructure and install more renewables.

Provinces & Climate Policy

As the picture painted above suggests, every government in Canada approaches the issue of climate policy with different economic and political interests — most of which are reflective of the composition of their domestic economy and the intensity of their respective emissions. When it comes to national climate policy, the key question is, which provinces have been the most motivated to intervene in the national policy process in order to protect those interests. While the provinces do indeed have a range of interests that cause them to either favour or oppose climate action, to date, the only ones that have taken aggressive action to influence federal policy are those that oppose action. In particular, the blocking role played by provinces like Alberta and Saskatchewan (and, to a lesser extent, Newfoundland and Nova Scotia) has created enormous difficulty, particularly when coupled with a general inclination among all provinces to fiercely protect their constitutional authority over things like natural resources, electricity, planning, agriculture, transportation, etc. As a result, Canada has generally lacked a California-like province willing to lead the charge on national climate policy, leaving willing governments in Ottawa somewhat vulnerable in their efforts to impose national regulations on unwilling provinces (see the final section of this chapter for some thoughts on how climate activists can use this knowledge to advocate for better policies).

ECONOMIC INTEREST GROUP #2: THE BUSINESS COMMUNITY

The interests of business and corporations are, in many ways, the same as that of states: they seek a stable and growing economy where they can expand and make greater profits. However, if a business wants to exist over the long term, it needs several other things as well, including policy certainty, investor confidence, and social legitimacy. As we'll see below, these competing demands have led Canadian businesses to take a variety of different approaches to the issue of climate change, all of which have proved enormously consequential to the trajectory of Canadian climate policy.

Why is business such an important player in climate policy?

When we look at the countries around the world that have succeeded at implementing strong climate policies, none have done so without the support of a large section of their domestic business communities (Christoff and Eckersley 2011). This is not coincidental. In a capitalist society, businesses tend, in most cases, to be the most powerful and influential players in policy development. This owes primarily to the fact that, in a capitalist society, business activity not only generates the jobs that employ the state's citizens, but it also creates the wealth that governments can tax to finance their militaries, police, courts, welfare states, and other public services — the combination of which provides states with their material power and legitimacy. In this context, the state is heavily reliant on the health and support of its business community, and most governments are loath to act without its support.

In addition to this structural reliance, the business community has some other key capacities that other groups do not have. Included among these are the ability to provide or withhold large donations to politicians and political parties, obtain privileged access to political officials through lobbying efforts, and spend large sums of money on advertising to gain public support for their policy objectives. Taken together, this makes the business community first among equals in the government's policy process.

Corporations & the environment

The relationship between corporations and environmentalism has been continuously evolving since the rise of the modern environmental movement in the 1960s. Caught completely off guard by the movement's meteoric rise, businesses in Canada were woefully unprepared to ward off the unprecedented spate of government regulations that ensued. As a result, the late 1960s through the early 1980s saw the creation of hundreds of new provincial and federal laws around everything from air and water quality, to waste disposal, wildlife, industrial and agricultural practices, mining, biological contaminants, inorganic and organic substances, various particulate matters, automobile emissions, and the management of public and private lands. Unprepared to deal with this type of challenge to their legitimacy and profitability, Canadian industry generally reacted quite defensively, viewing environmentalists as a threat to be overcome, and environmental standards as something to be weakened or prevented entirely (Macdonald 2009).

Beginning in the early 1980s, however, the business community's approach to environmentalism changed dramatically. Acknowledging that environmental values would be a permanent feature of Canadian life going forward, many industries and corporations sought to neutralize the regulatory threat by establishing voluntary codes of environmental conduct, signing memoranda of understandings with government regulators, and, perhaps most importantly, engaging in advertising campaigns designed to project a positive environmental image and ward off negative attention from environmentalists. Indeed, today it is extremely rare to find a Canadian business that does not at least *claim* to embrace the norms of environmentalism, regardless of what their actual environmental record may be.

Yet, while most Canadian corporations today will adapt to any environmental norm or standard that has low compliance costs (or which may even generate long-term savings and profits through enhanced efficiencies), corporations are still rational, profit seeking entities, and they will aggressively resist any regulatory action that they feel poses an existential threat to their core operations. In the case of climate policy, this is exactly what many elements of the Canadian business community have done over the past three decades.

A Brief History of Canadian Business & Climate Policy

As Macdonald (2009) notes, the majority of new environmental regulations imposed upon businesses throughout the 1970s and 1980s were generally seen as unwelcome, but rarely raised overall operating costs by more than 2 percent (and, as noted above, in many cases they actually helped to increase the efficiency and long-term profitability of many industries). Moreover, in most cases, Canadian businesses could be confident that similar laws were being established in competing jurisdictions, and thus there were minimal impacts on competitiveness.

Climate policy, however, struck many Canadian businesses (particularly those in high-emitting sectors) quite differently. While the wave of environmental regulations throughout the 1970s and 1980s were mostly, in effect, pollution control measures aimed at eliminating or managing the release of harmful *byproducts* from specific industrial processes, climate regulation took aim at one of the most crucial *inputs* to the economy as a whole — fossil fuels. For the oil, coal, and gas industries, in particular, climate policy effectively aimed to destroy them altogether. Moreover, in the case of climate policy, there was no guarantee that Canada's most important competing jurisdiction (the US) was going to implement similar regulations. Thus, taken together, climate regulation was something that many high-emitting Canadian businesses felt they could not abide. For many industries, this was not a simple pollution control measure that they could slowly integrate and use as a means to increase efficiency and profit over time. It was, in effect, an existential threat.

From the late 1980s through the late 1990s, the business community's strategy was fairly simple. Acknowledging that the provinces had jurisdiction over effectively every major GHG emitting activity in Canada, the main focus was on lobbying individual provincial governments to keep their climate ambitions modest, and to convince them to push for the weakest outcome possible in the National Action Plan on Climate Change process (NAPCC). Throughout this time, most industries sought to maintain their environmental legitimacy by acknowledging that climate change was indeed a problem and pledging to take voluntary measures to cut emissions through the NAPCC's resulting Voluntary Challenge and Registry program — duly acknowledging that it had no regulatory teeth whatsoever. With the exception of a few momentary hiccups (noted in Chapter 2) this strategy served the community well for most of this time, allowing them to appear willing and engaged on the issue, while knowing that the consensus driven NAPCC process would always tend toward the lowest common denominator and thus keep the threat of any serious regulation at bay. All of this changed in the early 2000s, however, when the Chrétien government decided that it was going to move forward with Kyoto's ratification and perhaps begin developing a substantive (and non-voluntary) regulatory program.

For the oil and gas sector in particular, the prospect of Ottawa unilaterally enacting federal climate regulations was arguably the most serious policy threat it had ever faced — perhaps even more so than Pierre Trudeau's National Energy Policy of the early 1980s. The industry thus opted to band together in an effort to not merely weaken or alter the federal plan, but to fundamentally upend it, and either replace it with a continental framework harmonized with the US (based on significantly weaker targets and longer time frames), or to simply destroy Ottawa's climate strategy altogether.

In the run up to the ratification vote in 2002, the oil and gas sector joined with a series of other heavy-emitting industries (e.g., automotive, construction, mining, transportation, utilities, etc.), multiple provincial governments (most prominently Alberta, but with general support from all provinces except for Québec and Manitoba), and several of the country's most influential business associations, (including the Canadian Council of Chief Executives, the Canadian Chamber of Commerce, Canadian Manufacturers and Exporters, and the Canadian Association of Petroleum Producers). Together, they undertook one of the largest efforts in history to undermine a federal policy initiative, using their unmatched financial and political resources to both directly lobby individual members of the government and launch a pervasive propaganda campaign aimed at turning average Canadians against climate action.

In the former effort, they spent millions of dollars trying to persuade elected officials that climate policy must only be developed in consultation with the provinces, that it must be fully consistent with US policy, and that the key policy mechanisms should be voluntary in nature (Macdonald 2009). In the latter effort, they argued in a series of radio, newspaper, and TV ads that ratifying Kyoto would cost the national economy close to a half-million jobs, raise electricity and gas prices for average workers and families, and make Canada significantly less competitive in the global economy.

Given the strength, organization, and determination of this effort, it is remarkably impressive that Chrétien managed to stick to his principled determination to see Kyoto ratified. This, however, would not be the case when it came to developing an actual strategy designed to meet Canada's Kyoto obligations. As noted in Chapter 2, the post-ratification climate policy debate would see the power of business restored, rendering it once again capable of disrupting any plans to develop or implement national climate regulations.

When & why did business begin to support a carbon price?

From the Kyoto ratification vote in 2002 until Stephen Harper's victory in 2006, federal efforts to develop a Kyoto implementation strategy effectively went nowhere. Too timid to unilaterally implement regulations, the Chrétien and Martin governments returned to provincial negotiations, where the business community reclaimed its enormous leverage over the process and regained its ability to bend the negotiations to its will. With the Conservative Party's victory in January 2006, it was clear that Ottawa, at least for the time being, was out of the business of climate regulation. For the business community, it appeared that, while they had lost the battle around Kyoto ratification, they had nevertheless won the war.

But by 2007, the business community had begun to change its tune. Whereas prior to 2006 most Canadian industries (particularly high-emitting ones) were generally opposed to the idea of climate regulation, the following years would see a majority of firms, sectors, and industry associations begin to openly support the idea of a *very small* price on carbon (see Tables 4.12 and 4.13).

Why did this occur? Interviews conducted by Munroe (2010) would tend to suggest that Canadian firms felt overwhelmed by the groundswell of support for climate action from mid-2006 through mid-2007, when national polling indicated that environmental protection had moved into first place on the list of most important issues for Canadian voters. With

TABLE 4.12 CORPORATE ASSOCIATIONS PREFERENCES
AROUND CARBON PRICING AFTER 2009

ASSOCIATION	SUPPORT CARBON PRICE?	SPECIFIC PREFERENCE FOR POLICY MECHANISM
Mining Association of Canada	Yes	Carbon tax
Canadian Vehicle Manufacturers Association	Yes	Cap-and-trade
Canadian Steel Producers Association	Yes	No preference
Canadian Gas Association	Yes	Carbon tax
Canadian Petroleum Products Institute	Yes	Carbon tax
Canadian Council of Chief Executives	Yes	Carbon tax
Canadian Chemical Producers Association	Yes	Cap-and-trade
Railway Association of Canada	Yes	Cap-and-trade
Forest Products Association of Canada	Yes	Cap-and-trade
Aluminum Association of Canada	Yes	Cap-and-trade
Canadian Association of Petroleum Producers	Yes	Cap-and-trade
Cement Association of Canada	Yes	Cap-and-trade

Source: Munroe 2010

the creation of a carbon tax in BC (and other provinces, along with the federal Liberal Party, considering similar measures), industry began to acknowledge that the era of climate policy stagnation was likely over, and that their best option was not only to come out in support of a carbon price, but to try to actively shape its development in order to make it as weak as possible.

For Munroe (2016), this decision is not terribly surprising, and is only confusing if we mistakenly assume that a corporation's only objective is near-term profit maximization. If indeed this were its sole objective, we would expect that a firm's only goal with regard to climate policy should be to minimize costs, and thus the only policy mechanisms they would be willing to abide are voluntary agreements and government subsidies — as indeed Canadian firms did from the late-1980s though the mid-2000s. But, in fact, Munroe argues that corporate climate preferences are also shaped by the need to manage certain risks in order to ensure their long-term survival — indeed, a firm cannot make profit if becomes insolvent and goes out of business. As the author notes, "When survival is perceived to be threatened, company officials adapt their decision-making to mitigate the threat and,

TABLE 4.13 CORPORATE PREFERENCES AROUND
CARBON PRICING AFTER 2009

FIRM	SUPPORT CARBON PRICE?	SPECIFIC PREFERENCE
Weyerhaeuser (forestry)	Yes	Cap–and–trade
Canfor (forestry)	Yes	Cap–and–trade
Catalyst Paper (forestry)	Yes	Carbon tax
West Fraser (forestry)	Yes	No preference
AbitibiBowater (forestry)	Yes	Cap–and–trade
Essroc (cement)	Yes	Carbon tax
St. Mary's Cement (cement)	Yes	Cap–and–trade
Holcim (cement)	Yes	Cap–and–trade
Lehigh (cement)	Yes	Cap–and–trade
Encana (natural gas)	Yes	Carbon tax
Union Gas (natural gas)	Yes	Carbon tax
Gaz Metro (natural gas)	Yes	Cap–and–trade
ConocoPhillips (petroleum)	Yes	Carbon tax
Suncor (petroleum)	Yes	Cap–and–trade
Nexen (petroleum)	Yes	Carbon tax
Petro–Canada (petroleum)	Yes	Cap–and–trade
Shell Canada (petroleum)	Yes	Cap–and–trade

Source: Munroe 2010

therefore, are more likely to support higher cost policies" (2010: 9).

One of the biggest threats to a firm's long-term survival is policy uncertainty and its impact on investment decisions. As the climate policy debate appeared to move from stagnation to calls for action in 2007, Canadian firms became increasingly nervous about the impacts that a strong carbon tax or "command-and-control" regulation could have on their internal investments. Indeed, if such a policy were to dramatically increase production costs, a facility previously amortized over twenty-five years could become unprofitable. This type of uncertainty is completely untenable for many businesses, as it becomes impossible to make calculated investment decisions.

In her study, Munroe (2016) notes that several oil companies operating in Canada were forced to delay the development of new projects because of uncertainty around climate policy after 2006. In particular, one company official from the multinational energy corporation Nexen noted that it was forced to put several Canadian projects on hold because of concerns about the possibility of onerous regulations emerging in the following years, either from specific provinces, or in the event that Harper's minority government was defeated. Company officials expressed concern that a high carbon price (developed without industry input) would make its projects and investments unviable, or even that they could be forced to develop a carbon capture and storage facility at the plant — a process that would dramatically change the profitability of the project.

Firms were likewise concerned about the perceptions investors might have about their company in the midst of this uncertainty. Indeed, if investors are nervous that an aggressive new climate regulation might ruin their investment, companies will be unable to raise the capital required to grow and expand. In particular, Munroe notes that a major oil sands project by TrueNorth was cancelled in 2006 for precisely this reason.

It was in this context that, just a few years after launching one of the largest campaigns in Canadian history to derail national climate regulation, heavy-emitting industries across the country (including groups like the Canadian Association of Petroleum Producers) came out in favour of a carbon price. In so doing, they aimed to create greater certainty around investment decisions (and, indeed, the very future of industries like oil and gas), and gain the legitimacy that comes from *looking like* an environmentally concerned corporation.

It is important to reiterate, as noted above, that the most important goal of this decision was to make sure that the resulting regulation would be a *very small* and manageable carbon price, not some form of onerous command-and-control regulation or prohibitively high carbon tax. The general idea is that if these major corporations and industry associations are at the table helping to draft climate legislation, it will be written largely on their own terms (see the final section of this chapter for some thoughts on how climate activists can use this knowledge to advocate for better policies).

ECONOMIC INTEREST GROUP #3: CANADIAN WORKERS

While it might be nice to think that environmental protection is a top priority for all Canadian workers, polls suggest that, just like for governments and businesses, average Canadians first and foremost want economic growth and stability. And they seek this for obvious reasons. When the economy is strong and growing, Canadian workers can generally expect greater job security, rising wages, and higher living standards for themselves and their families. Related to this, polls also suggest that workers want lower costs of living, lower consumer prices, lower taxes, and cheaper gasoline and energy prices. This is not a new or unusual finding. Since the rise of contemporary capitalism, this has been the basic trade-off for workers: endure a life of wage labour, and, in exchange, your living standards will, in theory, improve (see Chapter 6 for an environmental critique of this general logic).

In the context of modern industrial capitalism, environmentalism is sometimes referred to as a "post-material" value. That is to say, people will only really start to care about the environment (and consider making financial sacrifices for its preservation) once they have achieved a sufficient level of personal economic security (Clapp and Dauvergne 2005). Once this has occurred, the theory goes, an affluent and secure middle class will begin to insist on better environmental amenities like clearer air and water, and a safe and stable climate system. But the key question is, *how badly* do they want these things? What would they be willing to sacrifice for it? And how fickle are their commitments to these things as the national and global economies undergo their inevitable fluctuations? As we'll see below, while average Canadian workers claim a broad sympathy for the environment and the issue of climate change, their general willingness to make financial sacrifices for it is actually depressingly low. In this context, governments considering decisive action on these issues have, rightly, been extremely timid.

Opinions on the environment

In the half-century since the rise of the modern environmental movement, ecological values have become deeply ingrained in the fabric of Canadian life, influencing the way that individuals, families, and communities live, work, and play. Throughout this time, national surveys have consistently shown that a vast majority of average Canadians express deep sympathies for the environmental movement and are concerned about a long list of ecological issues, like air/water pollution, species extinction, habitat preservation, food safety, and climate change, just to name a few (see, e.g., Johnson and Bakx 2016; Ekos Research 2016; McCarthy 2017. Indeed, the data overwhelmingly suggests that Canadians are very worried about the environment, and, in general, are prepared to accept government regulation to address these concerns.

But, as Guber (2003) notes, polling on the desirability of environmental regulation changes dramatically when the questions shift from broad generalities to specific costs to be incurred by average citizens. As the author notes, "When confronted directly with the cost of protecting the environment — either through higher prices, increased taxes, or a reduction in the standard of living — consensus dwindles." In her study of American opinions towards environmental protection, Guber found that, while 61 percent of respondents thought the government should do more to address environmental problems, only one-third were willing to incur higher taxes to fund those efforts, and fewer still thought that it should take priority over economic growth or a series of other political and economic issues. Guber's findings tend to suggest that support for the environment is easier to achieve when polling questions do not contain specific prices and do not require choices between competing priorities and values.

On the issue of climate policy in Canada, surveys conducted by Lachapelle, Borick, and Rabe (2014) confirm Guber's findings. Individuals that initially indicated their support for carbon taxes, cap-and-trade, and/or renewable energy investment were then asked to state their level of support when those policies were accompanied by specified personal costs. As depicted in Figures 4.24, 4.25, and 4.26, while a decent portion of the Canadian population may see climate policy as being in their interest, there is an obvious tendency for that inclination to diminish when they are confronted with the specific costs of those policies — even if those costs are relatively minor.

In short, the overall message around Canadian workers and climate change is basically one of good intentions with no appetite for real sacrifice. To paraphrase Hal Rothman, if Canadians are environmentalists, they are half-hearted ones at best, and are unwilling to face difficult choices

FIGURE 4.24 CANADIANS' SUPPORT FOR A CARBON TAX

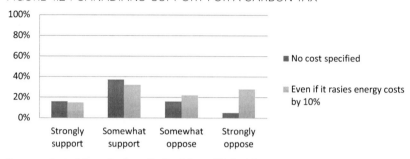

Source: adapted from Lachapelle, Borick, and Rabe 2014

FIGURE 4.25 CANADIANS' SUPPORT FOR CAP-AND-TRADE

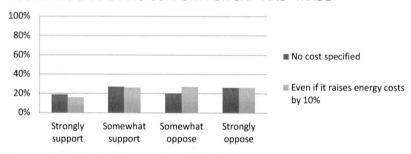

Source: adapted Lachapelle, Borick, and Rabe 2014

FIGURE 4.26 CANADIANS' WILLINGNESS TO PAY FOR RENEWABLE ENERGY

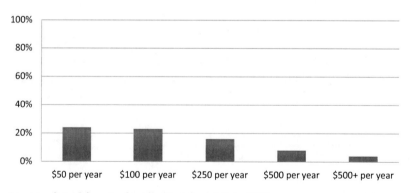

Source: adapted from Lachapelle, Borick, and Rabe 2014

or altered lifestyles. Why is this? Why are large swathes of the Canadian public so hostile to the idea of, for example, a small carbon tax, or even just paying slightly higher general taxes to fund programs designed to address climate change? To understand why support for environmental programs has become so weak, it is important to recognize how neoliberal reforms have repositioned anti-tax voting preferences as a basic economic survival strategy for many Canadian workers and families.

The past three decades in Canada have been a time of unparalleled deindustrialization and economic restructuring that has eliminated millions of previously secure middle-class jobs in manufacturing and middle management. As firms uprooted in search of cheaper operations in the developing world and new technologies displaced human labour, entire industries that once provided good-paying unionized jobs rapidly disappeared, replaced by low-wage, non-unionized, insecure positions in the service sector. Beyond manufacturing, this period has also seen big box retailers massively expand their reach in Canadian communities, decimating traditional retailers, mom-and-pop shops, and existing supply chains. To make matters worse, at the same time that millions of workers have lost access to employer-based benefits, government austerity measures have often meant that previously adequate social safety nets are overwhelmed and pared back.

The nature and extent of these dislocations in Canada has been well documented in a series of landmark studies. A generation ago, Gøsta Esping-Andersen (1990) had already begun to draw attention to the rapidly diverging trajectories of the neoliberalizing economies like Canada in his canonical work *The Three Worlds of Welfare Capitalism*, where he singled out Canada as offering some the weakest protections in the developed world from the impacts of the market. A decade later, Peter Hall and David Soskice's (2001) landmark book *Varieties of Capitalism* further underscored the accelerating pace of Canada's neoliberal trajectory. In their book, the authors note that the main institutional features of the Canadian economy (its employment contracts, training and education systems, unionization rates, income distribution, market regulations, etc.) were all increasingly reflective of a style of capitalism aimed at full commodification of workers and their conditions of survival.

Emblematic of this transition has been the hollowing out of good-paying manufacturing jobs (which have declined by more than 30 percent since 1990), a rapid pace of de-unionization (which fell from 48 percent of the workforce in 1975 to 30 percent in 2013), and a precipitous decline in real wage increases (with median earnings of full-time workers rising by only $53 between 1980 and 2010) (Government of Canada 2013; P. Harrison 2009). The OECD estimates, moreover, that Canada (along with other neoliberal states like the UK, US, Australia, and New Zealand) now feature the weakest protections against employee dismissal, as well as the most fluid and casualized labour markets in the OECD (OECD 2015).

While similar dislocations occurred across the Western world, neo-liberal countries like Canada are unique for the extent to which the Left has been overwhelmed by the pace of economic change and unable to match the strength of neoliberal rhetoric. When broadly compared with the rest of the industrialized world, mainstream institutions of the Left (progressive parties, social movements, welfare state institutions, etc.) have seen a particularly decisive decline. Across Canada, the main centrist and progressive parties have steadily moved to the near right, as their conservative counterparts successfully redefined the acceptable boundaries of the political spectrum (Peck 2001). Moreover, unions have not only decreased in density and instrumental strength, but have reflexively adopted strategies that are exclusionary, and rejected efforts to organize with poorly paid workers (disproportionately women, minorities, undocumented individuals, and youth) in casualized service sector posi-tions (Gordon 2007). The result is that unions, progressive parties, and social movements are increasingly seen as unable to provide a resolution to the economic insecurity faced by workers.

With the institutions of the Left in such poor health, the sense of injustice about bad jobs, low wages, and inadequate public services is increasingly unlikely to be expressed through collective mobilization against governments or corporations — nor is it expressed in a meaningful way at the ballot box, given the lack of faith in progressive parties. Instead, it is increasingly expressed through outright alienation from the politi-cal system, social institutions, and society more broadly. In many cases, however, it is expressed through reactionary opposition to policies seen as threatening the strategies that workers adopt to survive in a punitive, market-dominated society devoid of collective alternatives (Goldwag 2012). Put another way, as the Left has failed to frame economic insecu-rity in terms of a need for solidarity and collective institutions, workers have been compelled to adopt atomistic survival strategies. The result has been an explosion of anti-tax, anti-government, anti-immigrant, and anti-liberal elite politics from the same working-class communities that once strongly supported collective institutions in the postwar period (see, e.g., Frank 2004).

While these strategies ultimately fail to resolve the insecurity experienced by workers, there is an obvious logic and material basis to supporting them. In this equation, environmental policy actually looms very large. As public services decline (and as a greater share of the tax burden falls on lower-income earners, in line with supply-side economics), many resent having to fund a government that they feel does not represent their material interests. This anti-tax attitude is a natural response to a situation in which working-class solidarity is declining, public services are eroding, social mobility is declining, and plausible alternatives seem distant. The result is that tax resistance in Canada is effectively institutionalized, making it extremely easy to mobilize interests around low taxes, and difficult to build support for alternatives.

It is in this context that the weak support for carbon taxes and other climate programs needs to be understood. To the extent that opposition groups have, with exceptional ease, managed to frame such schemes as a tax hike on struggling workers, climate policy debates (with all their required nuance) tend to devolve into unwinnable debates over higher taxes. This has indeed been the case in Canada, where right-wing parties have consistently profited from framing carbon prices as a threat to the economic survival of working families.

Implications & Lessons for Climate Advocates

The key takeaway from this chapter is that states, businesses, and workers will not readily surrender their own wealth, prosperity, or financial security for the sake of climate action. This may seem obvious, but the failure to fully appreciate this simple fact has been at the foundation of Canada's climate policy failure for three decades. While some provinces, businesses, and communities are well-positioned to succeed in a post-carbon economy, others currently are not. And, as we have seen, groups that feel threatened by climate regulation are able to leverage key institutions and facets of Canadian culture to prevent it.

The sad part is that, if we are being honest, these groups have a right to be concerned. By any measure, Canada has a decidedly pitiful record of ensuring that major industrial transitions are managed properly. The hollowing-out of central Canada's manufacturing industry over the past few decades provides an instructive example, with working people and their families unfairly shouldering the burden of industry closure, losing stable, well-paying jobs and being forced into insecure work, long-term unemployment, and poverty.

Canada's rural oil, gas, and coal regions would likely feel the impacts of a poorly managed transition even worse. In these communities, such industries often comprise well over 25 percent of all employment, and, as these jobs tend to be the highest paid in the region, they represent the economic anchor of these communities, providing the economic stimulus for the entire local economy. For a preview of what would likely happen to these communities, one need look no further than the Appalachian region of the United States. In response to the introduction of sulphur dioxide restrictions in the early 1990s, coal-fired power plants across the US found it cheaper to start buying low-sulphur coal from the Mid-West, rather than install flue gas desulphurizers on their power stations and continue buying from Appalachia. As a result, companies in the region went bankrupt, workers lost their jobs, and local economies plunged into permanent stagnation. As this occurred, neither state nor federal governments stepped in to help these communities transition to a post-fossil fuel economy. Fast forward twenty-five years, and these parts of Appalachia have a poverty rate 44 percent higher than the national average, with more than half of households living below the poverty line. This economic crisis has, in turn, bred a social crisis, with rates of drug abuse, crime, and suicide in this region among the highest in North America (Greenblat 2016; Lowrey 2014).

In this context, climate advocates need to think very seriously about the sorts of planning and industrial strategies that will help vulnerable provinces, communities, and workers to thrive in a decarbonized economy. As discussed in Chapter 3, the process by which German governments helped to transition the country's coal regions over the past several years stands as a clear template. In this instance, federal and subnational governments invested billions of dollars in a highly methodical effort to locate new clean-tech industries in these states and communities, develop technology-hubs to help foster new knowledge-based industries, invest in large environmental and infrastructure projects aimed at cleaning up former mine sites, and fund new efforts to enhance tourism in the region. For workers employed in these industries, governments provided funding to support early-retirement packages for older coal workers, voluntary redundancy and transition payment schemes, and qualification training for displaced workers. The result was that these governments were able to successfully transition more than 100,000 coal workers, and build modern economies capable of thriving in a post-carbon world.

The German example shows that, if Canada is to do what is economically sensible, politically shrewd, and morally just on climate change, a central component will be looking out for the workers, communities, regions, and provinces whose economies will undergo the most dramatic restructuring. Since the mid-nineteenth century, these people have played an absolutely vital role in building and powering Canada's prosperity, and it would be intellectually dishonest and politically ruinous to throw these people on the scrapheap in pursuit of climate action. The German example suggests, moreover, that if managed properly, Canada's transition away from fossil fuels and high-emitting industries offers enormous opportunities for a strong economy not merely in the energy sector, but also in transport, construction, infrastructure, agriculture, and the service industry.

Indeed, with careful planning and targeted investment, Canada can work towards diversifying its economy and striving to be a world leader in a range of low-carbon sectors, including advanced manufacturing, information technology, biotech, medical engineering, education, and telecommunications — among many others. This is crucial not only for shifting employment away from high-emitting industries, but also for decreasing the relative economic and political strength of corporate actors in these sectors. As we saw above, these industries (particularly the fossil fuel sector) will fight aggressively to stop climate action — even shrewdly conceding in certain instances if they believe it will provide an opportunity to water down regulations. While one cannot simply make these corporations go away overnight, by taking deliberate efforts to diversify provincial and regional economies, their relative weight and power will gradually lessen, as will their influence over the policy process.

Finally, as we saw in the section on workers, while average Canadians are generally sympathetic to environmental issues, they typically will not support action if they perceive that they will be financially harmed by it. In this context, it goes without saying that there are obviously major structural changes that must be made to contemporary neoliberalism in Canada (see Chapter 6 for more on this). But if absolutely nothing else, current governments and policymakers must become infinitely better at designing and selling climate policies to average Canadians — many of whom are, at any given time, already struggling to make ends meet. Policymakers must design polices that avoid the appearance of a burdensome tax on struggling households, and take every effort to not only compensate families for higher heating, transit, and energy costs, but also make it absolutely clear to Canadians how these costs are being offset and how these policies are resulting in a better economy and cleaner environment. If this cannot be done, right-wing political parties will pounce and frame their anti-climate positions as a service to Canadian workers.

CHAPTER 5

IDEAS & CULTURE

Much like individual people, countries need an identity — something that makes them unique, special, and ties together an otherwise disconnected group of millions of strangers. Over the course of a country's history, a series of stories, traditions, and cultural practices emerge to play this binding role. Canada is no different. If anything, Canada arguably needs these ties more than many other countries, given that, in many ways, the country is a seemingly arbitrary line along the 49th parallel with no obvious or inherent connection between the people of St. John's and Victoria or any communities in between. Culture thus plays an enormous role in keeping Canada bound together. Whether it's the country's famed politeness, cold winters, scenic beauty, or just the fact that Canadians are happy to be distinct from (and smugly better than) their southern neighbour, these ideas are a crucial element of what it means to be Canadian, and they are an integral part of how the country thinks about itself and where it is going. As Marc Ross (2009) defines it,

> Culture provides a framework for organizing people's daily worlds, locating the self and others in them, making sense of the actions and motives of others, and for pre-disposing people and groups toward some actions and away from others. It does these things by organizing meanings, defining social and political identity, structuring collective actions, and imposing a normative order on politics and social life.

Of course, even when groups of people share a collective identity, it doesn't mean that these broadly held meanings are acceptable to everyone, or that each person will have the same ideas or expectations. Indeed, being part of the same culture merely means that we have a common conception of *how* the world works, not that we agree that this is how it *should* work. For this reason, intra-cultural battles over meaning and identity — and the ability to impose one particular set of cultural ideals on a given situation — are often the sites of some of the most heated and intense political battles.

Seen in this way, culture and ideas play an indispensable role in shaping a country's climate politics, as they inform the assumptions and beliefs people have about how debates should be framed, how specific actors ought to behave, and which policies can be considered legitimate. And, as we'll see in this chapter, Canada's cultural ideals have not been particularly helpful in generating a coherent and effective national climate strategy over the years. While most Canadians do believe that climate change is a serious problem (and that Canada must play a leadership role in the global battle against it), they are nevertheless hamstrung by a series of competing ideas about the nature of the Canadian economy, national prosperity, and environmental protection. As will be explored below, these competing ideas and narratives have made it extremely difficult to enact the complex reforms required in light of the climate crisis.

IDEA #1: CANADIANS' VIEWS ON CLIMATE CHANGE & SCIENCE

Among the most important cultural influences on climate policy is the question of how Canadians feel about the science of climate change and the need for action. This, it turns out, is a fairly complex question without a particularly satisfying answer. The good news is that, by and large, a significant majority of Canadians — roughly 80 percent — is convinced that the earth's temperature has indeed been rising over the past several decades (Lachapelle, Borick, and Rabe 2014). The bad news is that this seemingly strong consensus masks a series of caveats that actually make support for climate action rather shallow. Indeed, as we'll see in this section, while most Canadians generally believe in climate change and want to see action, it is not a particularly strong or durable priority for the electorate and can easily be pushed off the agenda.

The first, and arguably most important, caveat is to ask that 80 percent of Canadians if they believe the problem is human-caused or simply a natural variation in the earth's climate system. This turns out to be a crucial follow-up question, because if one accepts the reality of climate change but

FIGURE 5.1 CANADIANS' VIEWS ON THE CAUSE OF CLIMATE CHANGE

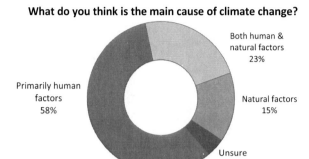

Source: adapted from Lachapelle, Borick, and Rabe 2014

is skeptical of its anthropogenic origins, then one is less likely to support policy interventions to remedy the problem. According to Glicksman (2010), this has been a major element of climate denial campaigns in the United States since the mid-1990s, as anti-climate groups found it more effective to simply deny global warming's anthropogenic origins than claim the earth is not warming at all. In the Canadian context, the news here is not great. As Figure 5.1 shows, of the initial 80 percent claiming to believe in climate change, only 58 percent believed the problem was primarily the result of human action. This would tend to indicate that, combined with the initial 20 percent of Canadians that simply do not believe climate change is occurring, there is a significant secondary segment of the population that remains either skeptical or confused about the role that humans have played in creating the problem.

This statistic is doubly disappointing when seen in a broader

FIGURE 5.2 CANADIANS' CLIMATE VIEWS IN GLOBAL CONTEXT

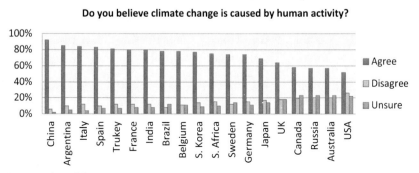

Source: adapted from Ipsos Mori 2015

FIGURE 5.3 VIEWS ON CLIMATE CHANGE BY PROVINCE/REGION

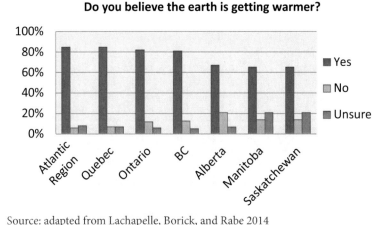

Do you believe the earth is getting warmer?

Source: adapted from Lachapelle, Borick, and Rabe 2014

international context. In countries where climate policy has succeeded, one can consistently observe an overwhelming belief among the population that climate change is both real and human-caused (Christoff and Eckersley 2011). Yet while Canadian views on climate science significantly outpace those of their American neighbours, the national consensus is actually very low by global standards, while the rate of climate denialism is alarmingly high (see Figure 5.2). Indeed, on this measurement, Canada resides among some of the world's pre-eminent climate laggards, like the United States, Australia, Russia, and Saudi Arabia.

A second caveat is to note that, while the country maintains a tenuous national consensus on climate change, views and opinions on the issue vary quite widely between regions and provinces. As Figure 5.3 indicates, in parts of Western Canada consensus can dip below 65 percent on the question of whether the planet is warming at all, suggesting that provinces like Alberta, Saskatchewan, and Manitoba have some of the highest rates of climate denialism on the planet. In some countries, this would perhaps just be a minor detail. But as we saw in Chapter 3, the nature of Canadian federalism furnishes these provinces with significant veto power on any national climate strategy. And as we saw in Chapter 2, these provinces have not been shy about using that power over the past three decades.

A third caveat would be to ask whether there is a general consensus on climate change among the country's major political parties. This is important because, as Christoff and Eckersley (2011) note, in countries that have made significant progress in battling climate change, elite political consensus (and a lack of inter-party disagreement) on the issue has been a crucial factor. Unfortunately, in Canada, there is no such consensus. As Table 5.1 depicts, on the question of whether the earth is warming at all, there is a significant gap between individuals identifying with right-wing political parties and those claiming allegiance to parties on the centre and left of the spectrum. Again, in some countries, this would perhaps be an inconsequential detail. But as we saw in Chapter 3, given the nature of Canada's first past the post voting system, these high levels of denialism among conservative voters and parties have a tendency to create insurmountable difficulties in the formal climate policy process.

TABLE 5.1 BELIEF IN CLIMATE CHANGE BY PARTY AFFILIATION

PARTY AFFILIATION	YES (%)	NO (%)	UNSURE (%)
Conservative	64	28	8
Liberal	91	6	3
NDP	84	10	6
Bloc Québécois	90	9	1
Greens	97	2	1
No party preference	80	13	7

Source: adapted from Lachapelle, Borick, and Rabe 2014

A final caveat would be to ask Canadians if climate change is not only real, but whether or not it is actually a serious problem that must be rapidly and aggressively addressed. This is a vital question given that there is a big difference between a passive, intellectual acknowledgment of a problem, and a passionate, whole-hearted belief that policy action and personal sacrifice is required. And, once again, the numbers are not encouraging. As Figure 5.4 depicts, a mere 32 percent of respondents who believed in climate change said they were "very concerned" about it, while 22 percent said they were either "not too concerned" or "not concerned at all." A plurality of respondents (41 percent) indicated that they were "somewhat concerned" — a response that politicians, rightly, interpret as apathy for the issue. As we saw in Chapter 2, this general lack of passion sends a clear signal to political leaders that they will neither be strongly rewarded for taking tough action on climate, nor strongly disciplined for failing to do so.

In short, while the fact that 80 percent of Canadians believe the earth

FIGURE 5.4 EXTENT OF CANADIANS' CONCERN ABOUT CLIMATE CHANGE

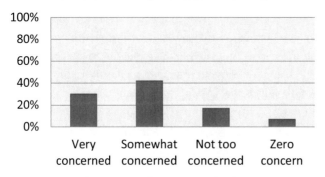

How concerned are you about climate change?

Source: adapted from Lachapelle, Borick, and Rabe 2014

FIGURE 5.5 ENVIRONMENTAL CONCERNS RELATIVE TO OTHER ISSUES

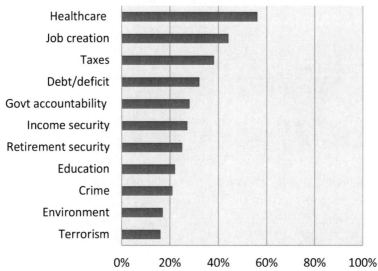

What are the top 3 issues in this election?

Source: adapted from Abacus Data 2015

is warming may appear to be a positive and hopeful sign, it nevertheless masks some important limitations. At the end of the day, climate change is not an overwhelmingly salient issue for most voters. While many Canadians claim a broad sympathy for the issue, that sympathy turns out to be rather shallow and flimsy, and can easily be quashed by more pressing issues. As Figure 5.5 suggests, in the run-up to the 2015 federal election, a mere 23 percent of likely voters were even willing to list the environment in their top three priorities — falling well behind perennial top-of-mind issues like the economy, taxes, and healthcare. The result is that, for most political leaders, the pressure to act on climate change is decidedly tepid.

Why Have Canadians Remained Ambivalent about Climate Change?

Nevertheless, that initial 80 percent of believers is not nothing. Indeed, one is often hard pressed to find any issue that 80 percent of the public can agree on. And, as we saw in Chapter 2, support for climate action can flare up at any time — recall in 2007 when it momentarily stood as the most pressing issue for a plurality of Canadians. In that context, one could still justifiably ask the question, if there is such a large percentage of the population that, to varying degrees, believes climate change is real, human-caused, and problematic, what explains the general lack of outrage about all the inaction over the past thirty years?

Part of the answer stems from what Canadians have generally been led to believe about domestic climate action from elite sources, in particular the federal government and national media. And on this score, the Canadian situation is rather unique and interesting.

According to Young and Coutinho (2013), unlike the US, where there is an extensive and well-documented climate-denial movement led by the fossil fuel industry, right-wing think tanks, conservative media, and corporate front-groups aimed at depicting climate change as a left-wing hoax, no similar domestic movement has ever really taken-off in Canada, where trust in such groups is considerably lower. Nor have conservative groups in Canada succeeded in breeding the type of hotly contested culture war around climate change that can be observed in the US, as Canadians tend, in general, to be less polarized than their southern neighbours on liberal vs. conservative cultural issues.

Instead, the authors argue that, in the main, right-wing political parties, think tanks, and media outlets have rejected the language of denialism, and strategically embraced an acceptance of climate science. This has turned out to be a brilliant strategy for those seeking to avoid action on climate. Whereas a brazen, American-style statement of denial would likely provoke a powerful backlash from a large portion of the electorate and elevate the issue's salience, "rhetorical acceptance of climate change opens up room for the construction of a 'trust bridge'" that allows people to be comfortable with inaction (Young and Coutinho 2013). Put simply, having been told for the past thirty years that Ottawa believes in this issue and intends to act on it, many Canadians have been left with the impression that the issue is slowly being addressed. This has opened up a whole new spectrum of possibilities for governments seeking to avoid acting on the issue.

While the Mulroney, Chrétien, and Martin governments made clear to Canadians that they believed in the issue and were trying to act on it, the more remarkable strategic efforts came from the Harper government — a government which, by all accounts, did not care at all for the issue. Despite this, Harper's government carefully avoided American-style denialism, and presented a skillfully scripted message of reluctant concern. Indeed, try as one might, it is nearly impossible to find a public statement from the Harper government espousing denialist views (some prominent members of the Conservative/Reform party expressed such views in the 1990s and early 2000s — Harper not least of whom — but after taking office in 2006, these sentiments basically ceased). In the rare instances where a statement was made that bordered on conventional denialism, the Prime Minister's Office quickly disavowed the comment and tidied it up.

For Young and Coutinho (2013), the Harper government managed the expectations of Canadians around climate change with a clever multi-pronged communications strategy that, in effect, threw most people off the scent for the better part of a decade. As the authors argue, this strategy had five basic components.

1. Compliance claims

With the exception of the Clean Air Act of 2006 (when the Harper government made clear that Canada's Kyoto targets would not be met), effectively all climate change communication from the government made use of what the authors call "compliance claims." Through this device, government reps consistently underscored that ambitious targets were being put in place, and that these benchmarks would be met in due time. Such statements were typically peppered with rhetoric and language borrowed directly from the environmental movement, such as when Environment Minister Jim Prentice vowed in 2008 that Ottawa is pouring "every effort into safeguarding all aspects of our environment against a force whose might carries with it consequences of potentially devastating proportions: climate change"; or in 2007 when Environment Minister John Baird acknowledged the growing calls for action on the environment and claimed "Canadians want action, they want it now and our government is delivering" (cited in Young and Coutinho 2013).

2. Competing priorities

A second key strategy was to continually underscore that, to a large extent, economic growth and environmental protection were "competing priorities." While the Harper government nevertheless claimed that they were indeed taking action on climate change, they were quick to remind Canadians that this required an incremental, sensible, and balanced strategy from Ottawa, so as not to destabilize the national economy. This messaging strategy proved particularly key in the government's attacks against Stephan Dion's proposed carbon tax in 2008, as well as debates around Bill C-288 — the 2006 opposition bill designed to legally oblige the government to meet Canada's Kyoto commitments. During these debates, the government argued that the bill would cost hundreds of thousands of jobs and rob Canadian families of thousands of dollars in income.

3. Exporting the problem

A third tactic (largely related to the previous one) was to suggest that Canada ought to wait until its largest trading partner, the United States, sorted out its own climate strategy. Particularly after the election of President Obama, this effectively became the Harper government's mantra on climate policy. Indeed, the government noted in most official climate communications that it would be tantamount to economic suicide to take action ahead of Washington. As noted in Chapter 2, Harper rightly acknowledged that the impossibility of passing national climate regulation through the US Congress would allow his "wait and see what the Americans do" strategy to amount to complete inaction for most of his tenure as prime minister.

4. Controlling the research message

While the anti-climate movement in the US actively sought contrarian scientists to lend credibility to their message, the Harper government resisted the temptation to follow suit. Instead, Harper chose to simply eliminate or scale back federal funding for several crucial networks for climate research in Canada, including the Canadian Climate Impacts and Adaptations Research Network, which was shut down after the government cleared its website of all reports and publications. Moreover, Harper established a policy at the Ministry of Environment that forbade any climate-related scientists from liaising directly with the media, instead requiring that all questions be answered in writing so that a Harper government official could vet their responses.

5. Shifting numerical targets

A final strategy used with great success was the ceaseless altering of government emissions targets in an effort to confuse and obscure Ottawa's action on climate. The government did this by continually altering the "base" and "target" years of Ottawa's commitments, as well as moving back and forth between the use of "total emissions" and "emissions intensity" as the goal of its policy — this latter move was particularly deceptive, as intensity targets allow for a rise in absolute emissions depending on economic growth (see Table 5.2). With each change, the scope of Canada's ambitions was typically reduced, but this was often hidden from the general public by the complexity of the language and an inability to keep

TABLE 5.2 SHIFTING FEDERAL CLIMATE TARGETS

COMMITMENT/ POLICY	BASE & TARGET YEARS	PLEDGED REDUCTION	PLEDGED REDUCTION RELATIVE TO 1990
Kyoto Protocol (1997)	1990 (base), 2012 (target)	6%	6% below 1990 levels by 2008–2012
Clean Air Act (2006)	2006 (base), 2020 (target),	20%	3% below 1990 levels by 2020
Turning the Corner (2007)	2006 (base), 2020 (target)	20%	3% below 1990 levels by 2020
Turning the Corner (2010)	2005 (base), 2020 (target)	17%	2.5% above 1990 levels by 2020
Paris Accord (2015)	2005 (base), 2030 (target)	30%	8% below 1990 levels by 2030

Source: adapted from Young and Coutinho 2013

up with the constant changes. In so doing, the government created the illusion of greater action, even if it had no intention of ever meting these meager (and purely aspirational) targets.

The Harper government's strategy of rhetorically accepting the need for climate action proved exceptionally useful at reducing public pressure for a coherent and effective policy for a few key reasons. First, it effectively masked the ideological motivations of the anti-climate movement in Canada. Unlike the US, conservatives in Canada were never drawn into a hostile cultural battle over climate science, and instead were able to make a compelling argument that they, in fact, had every intention of addressing this issue on behalf of the public. Moreover, where that promise was not compelling, they were able to make a seemingly pragmatic and rational argument that it would be imprudent to act before Washington had fully made a decision.

Second, the strategy was brilliant to the extent that it created an immense amount of ambiguous policy noise around climate change. In particular, the consistently changing emission targets, coupled with relentless promises about a potential emissions trading system and/or sector-by-sector regulatory approach, created signals that looked and sounded like action, even though they proved to be completely meaningless. This gave average citizens (who generally lack the time or capacity to decode this noise) the impression that meaningful action was being taken.

Finally, Young and Coutinho (2013) suggest that the true brilliance of this strategy has much to do with the specific way that the general public thinks about climate change as an issue. Sociological research on climate change shows that most people prefer not to think too much about the issue, because doing so is potentially scary and unnerving. As a result, most people will look for any possible way to de-problematize the issue so that it seems less severe and they can be excused from any further feelings of worry, guilt, or fear. The Harper government's strategy gave Canadians an opportunity to change the subject and not think about climate change because, indeed, Ottawa acknowledged the problem was real and had every intention of doing something about it.

Implications & Lessons for Climate Advocates

The key takeaway for climate advocates is that, while Canadians are indeed increasingly waking up to the reality of climate change, there still remains a *substantial* amount of work to do around disseminating proper information and educating the general public about the issue. Indeed, despite the fact that the scientific community reached a consensus on climate change many decades ago, activists unfortunately still need to focus significant attention and resources on public information campaigns designed to educate Canadians about both the basic science of global warming, as well as the real world social, economic, geopolitical, and security risks associated with inaction. As the polling data above suggests, these activities are needed most in the Prairie provinces, where ignorance about climate change remains alarmingly high, and the country's system of federalism allows governments there to create powerful roadblocks to a serious national climate strategy. A major shift in attitudes in this part of Western Canada would also go a long way toward prompting a broader change within the federal Conservative party, which has been able to use Canada's first past the post electoral system to give disproportionate power to groups that deny the reality of climate change. Finally, as the above discussion underscores, activists must also, unfortunately, dedicate substantial time and resources to exposing government strategies aimed at simply suppressing voter concern about climate change.

IDEA #2: CONCEPTIONS OF ECONOMIC PROSPERITY & COMPETITIVENESS

Another fundamental cultural factor influencing Canadian climate policy over the years has been the way that Canadians think about the country's economic prosperity. Broadly speaking, countries that have proved successful on climate policy (think of, for example, Germany, Denmark, Britain, Sweden, etc.) have all seen a similar idea gain prominence in their national discourse and imagination over the past couple decades. In the scholarly literature, the name for this discourse is "Ecological Modernization." As an idea, ecological modernization stands in opposition to the conventional assumption that there exists a zero-sum relationship between the economy and environment. Ecological modernization thinkers, by contrast, underscore the possibility of a reformed economy, one that would, in theory, be capable of facilitating a so-called virtuous fusion between economic growth and environmental recovery. In short, ecological modernization suggests that, with a fair amount of government assistance, modern economies can be readapted to promote more efficient and sustainable production processes that simultaneously create less waste and pollution, while at the same time generating increased economic growth and employment from the development of new markets in clean technologies and low-emitting industries (see, e.g., Braungart and McDonough 2002; Huber 2004; Mol 2001; Young 2000).

As noted above, these ideas have been most pronounced in Western Europe, where several states have, over the past couple of decades, begun to promote aggressive constraints on carbon emissions, while at the same time using government intervention (in the form of regulations on dirty industries, subsidies for emerging clean sectors, procurement spending for green technologies, etc.) to promote clean energy and industrial efficiency. In many of these countries, elites and policymakers have promoted ecological modernization ideas as an explicit strategy to enhance national competitiveness through greater industrial efficiency and domination of emerging markets in green energy, low-carbon transportation, cleaner industrial processes, and advanced materials. In these economies, ambitious climate policies have often been explicitly framed *not* as a regulatory burden on business, but rather as a competitiveness strategy, and as a means to promote a so-called third industrial revolution capable of generating powerful new waves of economic development and job growth.

Yet while ecological modernization ideas have indeed taken root in several major economies, Canada has not been one of them. Along with its Anglo-American cousins in Australia and the United States, Canada belongs to what Matthew Paterson (2009) refers to as a "carboniferous" bloc of countries, whose historical economic development has proceeded on the basis of cheap fossil fuel resources and extensive land development. For Paterson, many elites and policymakers in these countries have stubbornly clung to a historical idea that national competitiveness will continue to derive from an economic strategy based on unlimited extraction and use of fossil fuels.

Canada as a "staple resource" economy

The reason that this strategy has been so successful has a lot to do with deeply ingrained ideas about the nature of the Canadian economy and its prosperity. Indeed, an entire body of scholarly literature — referred to as the "staples paradigm" — has evolved over the years to describe the extent to which Canada's tradition of resource-led growth has left a lasting (and often negative) impact on the country's economy, institutions, and culture.

Dating back to the work of Harold Innis (1956) in the mid-twentieth century, the staples paradigm focuses on the crucial role that successive rounds of resource-led economic expansion have had in shaping Canada's domestic political and economic evolution, as well as the country's place within the global economy. These waves of development (beginning with cod fisheries, fur trading, timber, and agricultural goods, and later minerals and fossil fuels) were all heavily geared towards global export markets, and were primarily supported by foreign direct investment from colonial powers. As Hayter and Barnes (2001) suggest, this early notion of Canada as a limitless bounty of natural resources "fundamentally and indelibly stamped Canada from its very beginning as a particular kind of European geographical invention," and led to a pattern of European settlement in Canada "motivated by the desire to export staples to core countries."

For many writing in the staples tradition, this pattern of resource-led development contributed to a structural underdevelopment of the Canadian economy, creating an enduring dependence on resource exports and foreign investment, while directing attention away from the development of secondary economic sectors and home-grown innovation. A key reason for this was the marginal position that resource exports assigned to Canada in the global economy. Indeed, at the heart of staples theory is a discrepancy between the "centre" and "periphery" sites of the global economy, with the former standing as the major sites of innovation and production, and the latter serving as, in effect, resource bases to service the centre's development. As Canada's role as a peripheral resource economy evolved and was enhanced throughout the early twentieth century, the country's economic development occurred largely through the export of extractive resources and infrastructural investments to facilitate these activities.

With few exceptions, throughout Canada's early history public policy failed to break the pattern of resource-led development, foster the growth of domestic value-added industries, or otherwise attempt to use the country's immense resource wealth to support the growth of domestic innovation, manufacturing, or technological capability (and thereby foster Canada's own evolution into a centre site of the global economy). While Canada did eventually make strides towards sectoral diversification and the development of strong value-added sectors throughout the latter part of the twentieth century, the country's historic pattern of resource-led development (and the idea of Canadians as "hewers of wood and drawers of water") has continued to loom large in both national conceptions of self, and on the dominant economic interests these conceptions shape. This has particularly been the case since the late 1990s and early 2000s, when the Canadian economy began to experience a rapid and profound hollowing-out of its existing manufacturing and value-added sectors, and a return to a disproportionately large reliance on extractive resource exports (MacNeil 2014b).

The struggle to change the narrative

We can see that this conception of self continues to loom large in Canada's inability to embrace (or even modestly entertain) ecological moderniza-tion ideas. While leaders like Mulroney, Chrétien, and Martin made no systematic effort to champion ecological modernization discourse, Stéphane Dion was arguably the first to take up the challenge upon assum-ing the leadership of the federal Liberal party in 2006. Drawing on the type of rhetoric often used to sell ambitious climate policies in Western Europe, Dion promoted his national carbon tax by offering a reimagined version of the Canadian economy — one focused on green innovation, industrial efficiency, and dominance in environmental markets. As Dion argued,

> Already, Stats Canada estimates that the "green" business sector's annual sales are more than $26 billion, with employment at nearly a quarter of a million. These figures can only continue to increase if we focus on environmental action for economic competitive-ness. We can and must brand Canada as an international leader, committed to innovative products and services with environmen-tal quality. By marketing that brand, we can create a Canadian competitive advantage in export markets. (cited in Blair 2016)

But for all his effort throughout his tenure as Liberal leader, there is little evidence that Dion's framing found much national resonance (outside of some urban centres and progressive pockets of the country). As a counter, Stephen Harper appeared to have a profound understanding of the extent to which Canadians embrace the idea that Canada's prosperity is tied to resource extraction (especially oil), and developed a disciplined and systematic way of talking about it. In his 2016 study, Blair analyzed the public statements and speeches the Harper government made on environmental policy between 2006–2015, and identified three dominant themes regarding the relationship between resource extraction and the environment. Together, these themes constituted what Blair refers to as a "trade-off frame" between the two, implicitly designed to convey the message that a weak set of climate policies was Canada's only viable path to economic security.

The first theme was a set of normative arguments, expounded by Harper and all five of his environment ministers, contending that resource extraction and environmental protection were, by and large, mutually exclusive objectives, and that economic growth (particularly during a global financial crisis) must always be Ottawa's main priority. The second was a causal argument suggesting that implementing any climate policies more stringent than other large economies would harm the competitiveness of Canadian resources. This line of reasoning was initially focused on developing countries like China and India, but quickly switched toward the United States after 2009 when it became clear that Washington would struggle to develop any type of national climate regulation in the near future. The final theme was a follow-on causal argument suggesting that the entire Canadian economy would be seriously harmed as a result of declining competitiveness from strong climate policies.

Of course, conservative politicians have not been the only ones to promote these ideas about the nature of Canada's economic prosperity. Along with major elements of the country's business class, the national media has also played a key role. In a 2011 study, Laura Way used content and discourse analysis to look at the way that Canada's three largest newspapers (*The Globe and Mail*, *National Post*, and *Toronto Star*) framed their discussions about the Alberta tar sands between 2006 and 2011. She found that, with small exceptions, all three publications tended to reproduce the Harper government's general narrative regarding economic and climate policy, and, in particular, underscored the government's argument that Alberta's tar sands were rendering Canada an emerging energy superpower and that their continued cultivation was crucial for the national economy.

Justin Trudeau's seemingly bizarre decision to pair a national carbon price with a federally-sponsored expansion of tar sands pipelines (see Chapter 6) would seem to suggest that he acknowledged the power of this discourse. This decision — which has rightly infuriated many environmentalists across the country — shows an appreciation for the fact that, while a growing number of Canadians claim to support national climate regulation, they seem to remain inherently skeptical about the whole notion of ecological modernization in Canada. Indeed, while polls suggested in 2016 that a majority of Canadians supported Trudeau's proposal for putting a price on carbon, polls also indicated that a majority believed such a policy would make the country less appealing to business investment and create job losses, suggesting that Harper's narrative remains alive and well in the Canadian imagination (Canadian Press 2017).

Implications & Lessons for Climate Advocates

The key takeaway for climate advocates is that the nature of the Canadian economy is not simply dictated by the presence of certain natural resources or historical practices. Rather, it has much to do with the ideational frameworks and constructs that have been built around them, particularly by governments, media, and other elite elements in society. This means that, with enough effort, climate advocates can help to reframe this myth by reminding Canadians that the country's prosperity relies upon profoundly diversifying the economy and becoming a leader in clean energy, information technology, advanced manufacturing, medical engineering, biotechnology, and other high-value, low-emitting industries. As this age-old myth about Canadians as "hewers of wood and drawers of water" begins to fade, so too will the absurd notion that substantive climate policies will condemn the country to impoverishment.

IDEA #3: CANADA'S PLACE ON THE INTERNATIONAL STAGE

A final key cultural influence on Canadian climate policy — one that has actually played a positive role — is the way the Canadian public and federal policymakers conceptualize Canada's place within the international community. Perhaps more than most other countries, Canadians tend to take very seriously their international reputation and have deep-seated historical ideas about Canada as a good international citizen with an abiding commitment to cooperation and multilateralism. Indeed, polling data suggest that Canadians, by and large, take a great deal of pride in the perception (whether correct or incorrect) that they are a deeply revered nation on the global stage — one that stands up for what is right, participates in just wars, objects to unjust wars, supports multilateral institutions, accepts large numbers of refugees, and plays a pivotal role as a global peacekeeping force (Keating 2002). Particularly when compared with the complicated reputation of their American neighbours, Canadians typically delight in their sterling international status, and generally want to see Ottawa live up to this reputation on a range of global issues.

To a large extent, this mythology of "Canada the good" helps to explain the relentless push for a functional national climate policy, as well as the incorrigibly hopeful rhetoric that has accompanied Ottawa's failures on the issue. As Harrison (2006) notes, many of Ottawa's actions on climate change over the years — particularly its seemingly progressive moves, like its decision to accept a larger than expected emissions target at Kyoto, or its decision to ratify the protocol despite the enormous difficulty of achieving compliance — cannot be explained by traditional political science theories that focus primarily on material self-interests and institutions. Rather, in these contexts, Ottawa appears to have been proceeding on the basis of a set of ideas about Canada's proper historical conduct on the global stage. And while Canada has continually failed to actually implement any substantive national policies aimed at addressing climate change, it is arguably these cultural ideals that have kept Canada engaged on climate policy over the past three decades.

"Good international citizenship" & the Canadian public

Prior to the Second World War, Canadian foreign policy could be described as relatively quiet and unambitious, with Ottawa typically residing in the long shadows of its American and British cousins for most of its early history. Following the war, however, Canada rapidly emerged as a leading "middle power," carving out positions that were increasingly independent from the US and UK, and developing a prominent role in shaping the post-war global order through its role as a mediator and moral leader. Indeed, throughout the 1940s and 1950s, Canada rose to great prominence through its key roles in constructing several multilateral institutions (the United Nations not least of which) as well as its powerful diplomatic corps, which quickly established a reputation for promoting international cooperation. Among the more notable early achievements was the success of Foreign Affairs Minister (and future Prime Minister) Lester Pearson in spearheading the development of UN peacekeeping forces, as Canada took a lead in pacifying the Suez Canal Crisis in 1956.

In the succeeding decades, Canada not only forged a leading role as a peacekeeping force — deploying thousands of soldiers under UN authority around the globe — but also led the way on a series of progressive global agreements, including the Montréal Protocol on ozone depletion and the Ottawa Convention on the use of anti-personnel mines, among many others. As Keating (2002) notes, this notion of Canada as a "good international citizen" — one that facilitates peace, cooperation, and progress around the world — has become a fundamental aspect of the Canadian identity. "These accomplishments have contributed to the Canadian identity, to our sense of ourselves as a people and as a community in the wider world." Indeed, whether it is completely accurate or not, this notion is deeply embedded in how Canadians conceptualize their place on the global stage, and how they expect Ottawa to act on their behalf (for a more honest and critical account of some of Canada's actions on the global stage, see, e.g., Gordon 2010; Gordon and Webber 2016).

In the context of global climate governance, survey data show a clear desire among Canadians to continue to play this role. Lachapelle, Borick, and Rabe (2014) found that a strong majority of Canadians believe Ottawa should be an international leader on the issue, with 80 percent of respondents agreeing that Canada should lead the way on emissions cuts (see Figure 5.6), and 75 percent suggesting that Ottawa should do so even if other major countries refuse to do likewise (see Figure 5.7). This marks a strong contrast with Canada's southern neighbours in the US, where only 57 percent of respondents believed Washington had a responsibility to lead, and a mere 52 percent thought the US should accept cuts even if other major emitters refuse to do likewise.

Acknowledging this to be the case, most prime ministers have been eager (at least in terms of rhetoric) to live up to this expectation. Brian Mulroney, for his part, appeared to be deeply aware of the good

FIGURE 5.6 CANADIAN'S VIEWS ON GLOBAL CLIMATE LEADERSHIP

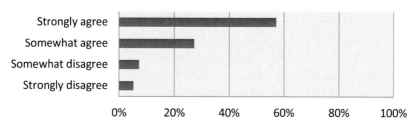

Does Canada have a moral obligation to show global leadership on climate?

Source: adapted from Lachapelle, Borick, and Rabe 2014

FIGURE 5.7 EXTENT OF CANADIAN'S SUPPORT
FOR A GLOBAL CLIMATE TREATY

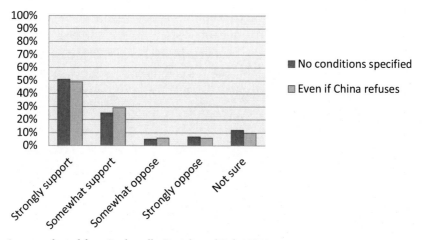

How much do you support Canada signing a global agreement to limit GHG emissions?

Source: adapted from Lachapelle, Borick, and Rabe 2014

international citizen narrative — and the importance of playing it up for domestic consumption — when his government took the lead in hosting the 1988 Toronto Conference on climate change and made Canada the first industrialized country to ratify the UNFCCC charter. Following suit, Jean Chrétien and Paul Martin rarely missed an opportunity to play up this idea, continually invoking the country's historical tradition of leadership on a range of environmental and geopolitical issues, and pledging to build on this heritage through leadership on climate. Of course, as noted in Chapter 2, the claims of Mulroney, Chrétien, and Martin were all undermined by the dramatic rise in GHG emissions during their respective tenures, as well as their questionable commitments to the UNFCCC process itself. Nevertheless, their rhetoric played perfectly to this deeply held belief in Canada's global benevolence, and signaled to Canadians that Ottawa intended to reaffirm the country's position as a proud global leader on the issue.

The Harper government was really the first and only administration to openly reject this idea, and it arguably caught up with them over time. From the start, Harper's intention was to fashion his government as the "honest truth tellers" about climate change and the UNFCCC, contrasting itself with the dishonest and empty promises of the Chrétien/Martin Liberals. Harper rejected any notion that the industrialized world had a historical responsibility for climate change, and made it clear that Canada would not take the lead in reducing its emissions, but rather wanted other countries (particularly the US, China, and India) to lead the way. Indeed, Harper's Conservatives largely rejected the idea of Canada as a golden child of the international community, and sought to construct a new idea of Canada as a tough and unyielding international force. Nevertheless, while Harper may have been more honest about his position than his predecessors, polls suggest that he was decidedly unsuccessful in developing a different narrative about Canada's place in the world (Paris 2014), and that he badly misread this crucial ideational aspect of the Canadian identity. Polls suggested that, near the end of his tenure in office, Canadians were overwhelmingly disappointed by his government's perceived lack of global leadership on climate (Lachapelle, Borick, and Rabe 2014).

While there is perhaps a great deal of value in Harper's efforts to expose the myth of Canada's good international citizenship, his successor, Justin Trudeau, seemed keenly aware of the extent to which Canadians delight in this myth. This was clear in the way that Trudeau spoke about climate change on the 2015 campaign trail, largely eschewing conventional rhetoric about building a green economy or intergenerational justice, and instead focusing heavily on the global shame that Harper had brought to Canada's once-proud reputation, and happily restoring the glowing Mulroney/Chrétien/Martin rhetoric about the need for Canadian leadership. This was also clear in a series of early efforts by the Trudeau government at COP 21 in Paris, where the Canadian delegation increased funding promises for the Green Climate Fund and pushed for a 1.5°C as opposed to 2°C target in the Paris agreement.

"Good international citizenship" & government strategy

Ideas about Canada as a good international citizen has an elite component as well. In particular, "multilateralism" has, for the better part of seventy years, been a key way that federal policymakers have conceptualized Ottawa's foreign policy goals (Black and Donaghy 2010). Over the past several decades, Canada has earned a reputation for being one of the most well-connected countries in the international community, having joined and played a founding role in countless multilateral institutions, ranging from massive organizations like the UN, to small regional clubs like the Arctic Council (Keating 2003). The depth of this commitment has been on display in numerous instances over the years, most notably in Ottawa's refusal to send forces into Iraq in 2003 without approval of the UN Security Council. In this instance, so strong was Ottawa's commitment to multilateralism that it yielded its national policy to a Security Council on which it didn't even possess a seat.

Why does Ottawa care so much about multilateralism? There are, of course, all the standard reasons one would normally imagine — for example, that through the use of negotiation and compromise, multilateralism helps to promote a rules-based global order in which many countries can flourish in a peaceful, secure, and economically prosperous environment. But for Canada specifically, multilateral institutions allow Ottawa to exert an influence over global affairs that is disproportionate to its economic and military power. While Canada lacks the capacity to bend others to its will through the exercise of hard power, these institutions (and Canada's reputation within them as a tireless diplomatic force and consensus builder), have allowed Ottawa to shape geopolitics according to its own goals and values. In this context, the idea of multilateralism (and productive participation and cooperation in multilateral institutions) has stood as the bedrock of Canadian foreign policy for seven decades.

Given the enormous geopolitical benefits that have accrued to Canada via multilateralism, federal policymakers have naturally maintained a powerful inclination to be a productive member of the UNFCCC — an organization that is emblematic of multilateral norms. While the influence of this inclination can be seen throughout the history of Canadian climate policy, the most vivid display likely came in the run-up to the Kyoto negotiations. Previously unengaged on the issue, Jean Chrétien became highly sensitive to the growing condemnation from NGOs and partner states about Ottawa's lack of action, and quickly assumed a more hands-on role. As we saw in Chapter 2, his eleventh-hour intervention, in which he unilaterally increased Canada's emissions target to avoid falling behind the US, was done at enormous domestic political risk, as he scrapped his agreement with the provinces without any consultation. As one Cabinet official noted, "Chrétien did not like to be told by other leaders, especially other progressive leaders, that Canada wasn't doing its share... if Japan was going to do it, he would do it; if Europe was going to be there, he would be there" (cited in Harrison 2006).

Why hasn't Canada lived up to these ideals?

Yet despite the strength of these ideas about Canada's role on the international stage, Ottawa has continually failed to live up to them in the context of climate change. While the Harper era may have marked a jarring break with these ideas and traditions, the picture painted in Chapter 2 suggests that Harper's approach actually showed a fair amount of continuity with his predecessors. Whether working as part of JUSCANZ to prevent binding international targets, or attempting to build numerous loopholes into the Kyoto Protocol to water down the treaty, or, indeed, ratifying an international protocol that it knew was impossible to achieve, Ottawa has consistently acted contrary to these supposedly deep-seated ideas. Why?

The problem with trying to proceed on the strength of ideals alone is that they are often not enough. While they can exert great pressure on governments to behave in certain ways, they rarely overpower the strength of material interests or institutional dysfunctions. And, as we saw in the preceding chapters, these material interests and institutional dysfunctions are indeed formidable. When seemingly willing governments like Mulroney's, Chrétien's, and Martin's attempted to live up to these ideas about Canada's role in the world, they were quickly confronted by a powerful coalition of provinces, industries, and voters that stood to incur losses from it. Moreover, negotiations with these groups occurred in an institutional context that made it nearly impossible to make any significant headway.

Put simply, Canada's commitment to multilateralism has always been more of a preference than a guarantee, and this type of pragmatic deviation from it is nothing particularly new. While Ottawa has undeniably been a strong defender of multilateralism over the past seven decades, it has nevertheless abandoned the practice on several occasions when it has not suited the national interest. In many instances, Ottawa has simply opted to follow the US on a variety of issues around security or economics, thereby challenging its multilateral commitments. Moreover, it is worth noting that being a staunch multilateralist is arguably a much heavier lift today than it was during the early post-war period when Ottawa began to establish this reputation, with the number of international treaties tripling since the 1970s, and the number of global institutions increasing by more than two-thirds since the 1980s. In this context, the demands for compliance with internationally determined standards in a variety of policy areas is considerably greater than it once was, and can create enormous strains for countries like Canada that seek to be a good team player with as many of them as possible. Kyoto, in this context, may simply have been an instance where Canada's optimistic multilateralist rhetoric and style caught up with it, and, instead of acknowledging that the country's political, economic, and institutional realities were too powerful for Ottawa to be an early champion on the issue, several leaders tried in vain to proceed on the basis of ideals alone.

At the end of the day, ideals are, at best, a complementary factor that can influence and drive policy decisions in progressive directions, but they are rarely the most powerful force in the equation. Nevertheless, the fact that, after thirty years of embarrassing failures, Ottawa still tries to redeem itself within the UNFCCC may be the greatest testament to the strength of these ideals.

Implications & Lessons for Climate Advocates

The key takeaway for climate advocates is that, at least for the time being, this is perhaps the most powerful force driving Canadian climate policy forward, and thus, it ought to be capitalized upon wherever possible. Given that many Canadians remain blissfully unaware of Canada's villainous standing within the UNFCCC (indeed, as noted in Chapter 2, Canada is easily one of the world's most loathed climate pariahs), activists should focus attention and resources on educating the public about the extent of the shame and condemnation that has come to Canada's good name over climate change. A keen understanding of this indignity among the electorate can, under the right circumstances, place heightened pressure on governments to act.

CHAPTER 6

WHERE TO FROM HERE? TRUDEAU'S CLIMATE POLICY & BEYOND

In late 2016, the Trudeau government negotiated the largest and most comprehensive national climate strategy in Canada's history. Referred to as the Pan-Canadian Framework on Clean Growth & Climate Change the accord was signed by every province and territory (save for Saskatchewan), and contained a series of new programs never before seen at the federal level in Canada. This included, among other things:

- a requirement that all provinces and territories establish either a cap-and-trade system or carbon tax of at least $10 per tonne of CO_2 by 2018, and increasing by at least $10 per year to reach $40 per tonne by 2022;
- a Low Carbon Fund of $2 billion to support projects by provinces and territories, municipalities, businesses, and Indigenous governments and organizations that reduce GHG emissions and contribute to clean growth;
- regulations to help accelerate the phase out of coal-fired power plants by 2030;
- new performance standards for natural gas electricity plants;
- policies to reduce emissions from chemicals and nitrogen fertilizers;
- new fuel standards to reduce emissions from transport, buildings, and industry;
- new fuel economy standards for light- and heavy-duty vehicles.

Relative to the previous quarter-century of federal inaction, this agreement was clearly a positive development, and, if fully implemented, could result in some much needed policy-induced emissions reductions. However, based on the analysis set forth in this book, there is good reason to be concerned about the technical efficacy and long-term political viability of the Trudeau government's approach. This chapter considers three reasons why this strategy is unlikely to be particularly effective and provides some preliminary insights on alternative ways forward.

1. Ottawa's plan is based on exceedingly weak targets

The first major cause for concern is that, despite these renewed efforts, the Trudeau government refused to increase the ambition of Canada's GHG targets beyond the Harper government's remarkably low goal of 30 percent below 2005 levels by 2030 — which independent scientific analyses have deemed "highly insufficient" (Climate Action Tracker 2019; Burck et al. 2018). (It is worth noting that this target is significantly weaker than Canada's initial Kyoto commitment of 6 percent below 1990 levels, given that Canada's emissions had increased substantially by 2005). Indeed, this commitment places Canada well towards the back of the pack among its peer nations and is not remotely consistent with the international community's goal of limiting global warming to 1.5°C. Rather, if all countries took on the same relative target as Canada, it is estimated that the planet would lock-in warming of up to 4°C, thereby guaranteeing a state of "runaway climate change" (ibid.).

In short, even if the Trudeau government's policies could be helpful in allowing Canada to reach its Paris target (which, at the time of writing, remains a lofty challenge), the target itself is *pitifully low*. If Ottawa is serious about being an international leader, a target of *at least* 50 percent below 2005 levels by 2030 would be required. Moreover, as part of the package of policy measures designed to reach this target, the government has included the purchase of international carbon credits (which means that many of Canada's reductions will not be the result of domestic mitigation efforts), but Ottawa has not specified how many credits they plan to purchase.

2. The deal is extremely politically fragile

While this book was in the final stages of drafting, much of Ottawa's fragile climate accord came unglued as the crop of twelve pro-climate premiers that initially signed the treaty with "handshake commitments" came to be replaced by reactionary conservative leaders. In mid-2018, Ontario became the first province to walk away from the accord, as PC Premier

Doug Ford skillfully framed the previous government's climate initiatives — particularly its cap-and-trade program — as a burdensome tax on struggling workers and families (it is worth noting, of course, that 60 percent of Ontarians voted for parties that supported climate action, but under the FPTP electoral system, these parties won a mere 38 percent of seats in the legislature). In 2019, Alberta's newly elected United Conservative Party followed suit, vowing to scrap the province's carbon tax as its first legislative act. As a result, by mid-2019, a group of provinces representing more than 75 percent of Canada's emissions profile (Saskatchewan, Manitoba, Ontario, and Alberta) had become non-compliant with the treaty, threatening to make the whole exercise effectively worthless. With its hand forced, the Trudeau government made the impressively bold decision (given the history of Canadian federalism noted in Chapter 3) to unilaterally impose a carbon price on these provinces.

At the time of writing, it remains unclear what the final outcome of this action will be, as these provinces and the federal government remain locked in a bitter legal battle over Ottawa's constitutional ability to make such an imposition. What is clear, however, is that Ottawa faces an enormous challenge trying to maintain the policy's popularity over the coming years. Opposition will be relentless at the federal level as well, where Conservative leader Andrew Scheer has continued his Party's staunch opposition to a carbon price — a strategy that proved effective in the 2008 election when the Liberals, under Stéphane Dion, campaigned on the creation of a carbon tax. Referring to Trudeau's plan as a "cash grab" and a "job killing measure," Scheer has vowed to scrap the accord, and will undoubtedly make opposition to a national carbon price a key theme of subsequent federal elections.

All of this serves as a timely reminder that, if Ottawa fails to clearly highlight the economic and environmental value of these initiatives for voters, conservative parties can (and will) stoke a powerful backlash against them for their own electoral benefit. At the time of writing, this messaging is not going terribly well. Polling suggests that most Canadians are rather confused about Ottawa's climate strategy — few understood at all what a carbon price does or how it works, and most believed it would make the country less appealing to business investment and raise costs for average families (Canadian Press 2017).

In short, it remains rather unclear if the current plan will even last long enough to achieve full implementation, much less become popular enough to be institutionalized and strengthened in future years. The near-term trajectory for this strategy will inevitably be one where the Trudeau government is involved in an awkward balancing act to shore up a weak climate accord against the enormous challenge of skittish provinces, anti-tax ideology, and a growing populist backlash against climate policy.

3. Trading carbon prices for pipelines is not a path to decarbonization
It should seem glaringly obvious (even to an uninformed observer), but it is worth stating without equivocation that Canada *cannot* simultaneously promote the expansion of its oil sector *and* the decarbonization of its economy. Given the medium-term goal of full decarbonization (which, in rich countries like Canada, has to be arrived at long before 2050 if 1.5°C of warming is to be avoided), coal, oil, and natural gas consumption has to be *fully eliminated*. And it should go without saying that the first oil to be eliminated will have to be tar sands oil, given its costs in both financial and CO_2 terms.

At the moment, oil and gas process emissions (i.e. *not* including consumption) represent a quarter of all Canadian emissions. Thus, any strategy for full decarbonization must include abandoning that sector over time. But even 80 percent cuts (the most ambitious targets currently being pursued by large industrialized economies like the UK and Germany) would mean there could be *no growth in this sector*, and all other sectors would have to rapidly fall to zero emissions. Building and expanding oil pipelines as a means to gain compliance from oil-exporting provinces not only promises to increase Canadian emissions in the short term, but it locks them in over the longer term, as the industry will have the infrastructure required to keep pumping oil for as many decades as possible. Put simply, trading carbon prices for oil pipelines is an absurd strategy and must be called out as such.

WHAT WOULD A SERIOUS CANADIAN CLIMATE POLICY LOOK LIKE?

The reality is that there is no set script for how Canada ought to move forward on climate policy. Different jurisdictions around the world have successfully employed many different strategies tailored to their local conditions, and one could think of any number of specific policies that could be adapted to the Canadian setting. But in broad terms, it would seem that a least a few general things would be required in a serious and effective strategy.

First and foremost, as noted above, it would require a strong and committed set of policies designed to begin immediately winding down Canada's oil and gas sector — complete with a host of policies designed to help governments, communities, and workers in fossil-fuel rich provinces like Alberta, Saskatchewan, Newfoundland & Labrador, New Brunswick, and Nova Scotia develop new industries and livelihoods capable of replacing the role that fossil fuel extraction and exports have played over the years. The first symbolic step by both federal and provincial governments would be to immediately eliminate all government subsidies to the fossil fuel industry, which cost Canadian tax payers an average of $3.3 billion per year (International Institute for Sustainable Development 2016). This money could be redirected to helping fossil fuel regions diversify their economies through, for example, job and retraining programs, and incentives to build and locate new industries there.

As we saw in Chapter 4, a significant portion of Canada's carbon emissions come from the transportation sector, and thus a serious plan would require a coherent strategy to begin immediately weaning the nation's vehicle fleet off of fossil fuels. This would entail, if nothing else, an explicit early target date for ending the use of gasoline and diesel in vehicles (along the lines of those announced by France, the UK, and others), coupled with massive government-led investments in electric charging infrastructure for the country's cars, trucks, and buses.

Related to this, a serious strategy would involve massive government-led investments designed to rapidly bring the nation's electricity sector to zero emissions over the next handful of years. This would mean investing tens of billions of dollars (as opposed to the currently proposed $2 billion) in installing new wind, solar, and storage technologies in provinces that still rely heavily on fossil fuels for their electricity generation.

A serious plan would include a calculated strategy to fundamentally reshape the places where we live and work. This would mean immediately implementing radically improved building codes to require zero emissions from all new homes and buildings (equipping them with, for example, state of the art insulating technologies, low-emissivity windows, renewable energy installations, etc.), and major government-led investments to oversee extensive retrofitting of existing ones. It would require drastic changes in urban planning to increase density and make public transit, cycling, and walking integral to municipal transport systems.

While upsetting for many Canadians, a serious climate policy would also require a radical challenge to the country's diets, where beef and other GHG-intensive meats are central. This remains one of the most unpopular aspects of climate policy around the world — indeed, even leading climate nations have struggled to address this particular issue, and have been loath to even consider the concept of a "meat tax" or other forms of regulation. But, if nothing else, this would require a national strategy to immediately begin disseminating better information about the threat that meat consumption poses to the climate (and, for that matter, human health and animal rights), and major government investments in urban agriculture, fresh/local food production, and the broad uptake of plant proteins in Canadian diets. Failing this, Canada will remain among the highest per-capita meat consuming countries on the planet.

Perhaps most importantly, it would require a broad rethinking of Canadian industrial policy, featuring a plan to develop an economy in which fossil fuels do not play such a large role in generating the country's wealth. This would mean extensive government-led investments in R&D, advanced manufacturing, clean-tech, and a range of low-emitting sectors like healthcare, education, and low-carbon agriculture.

CAN CANADA'S CURRENT SET OF INSTITUTIONS, IDEOLOGIES, & ECONOMIC INTERESTS ACHIEVE THIS?

Put simply, it would appear that they cannot. As argued throughout this book, while the actions of certain political leaders have clearly been unhelpful over the past thirty years, the real problems with Canadian climate policy are inherently more structural in nature. This means that the resolution will entail much more than replacing a given prime minister, premier, or mayor at the next election. Rather, it will require a *radical* challenge to Canada's reigning institutions, ideologies, and economic structures. The specific points laid out in each of the preceding chapters provide a good sense of some of the specific targets on which climate advocates ought to focus. But I want to close the book by highlighting what may be the single most important structural roadblock to a functional and effective national climate policy.

The problem with neoliberalism & climate policy

Underpinning much of the dysfunction noted in this book is the reigning political–economic paradigm referred to as neoliberalism. As a policy principle, neoliberalism prescribes that, to the greatest extent possible, governments and other democratic institutions should be rolled-back so that free markets and private businesses can solve all of society's major social and economic ills (see, e.g., Harvey 2007; Peck 2013; Saad-Filho and Johnston 2005). Since the early 1980s, the impacts of this doctrine on Canadian society have been hard to ignore. It is this set of governing principles that have seen governments across Canada rollback basic protections for workers; make cuts to important social programs like healthcare, childcare, and education; increasingly shift the tax burden away from large corporations and on to working Canadians; privatize crucial national industries and government capacities; and dramatically reduce regulations around the environment, labour rights, and consumer safety.

Neoliberalism's impact on climate policy has, likewise, been on full display for the past three decades. It can be seen in both the tendency of governments across Canada to completely avoid climate action for almost twenty years in an effort to appease the business community, as well as the types of "market environmental policy" that most eventual responses have taken. And on this latter point, it is worth being unequivocal about the general value of these programs. By pretty much any metric, the neoliberal/market-based approach to climate policy that has dominated over the past generation has been an *abject failure*. The notion that solving this problem could be as simple as putting a small price on carbon and letting the market "take care of the rest" has proved to be a political and environmental disaster. Indeed, this has been the central policy approach around the world for the past quarter-century (see, e.g., Paterson 2012; Spash 2010) and the results are plain to see. Globally, emissions are *not* falling at anywhere near the rate required to avoid a climate catastrophe, and (despite the promises of free-market economists) levels of private-sector investment have remained far too low to create the required transition to a low-carbon future. According to the International Energy Agency, the annual investment deficit in low-carbon technologies is close to one trillion US dollars annually and shows no signs of improving anytime soon (IEA 2016).

The reason for this is obvious: there is simply not enough immediate profit in low-carbon technologies to attract the levels of private capital required, and there is no politically-palatable carbon price high enough to change that calculation for the private sector. As a result, the majority of investments that *have* materialized to date have come from public funds, mostly through government subsidies and concessionary lending (Sweeny and Treat 2019). In short, the neoliberal approach has not only failed to deliver the promised results, but it has, in effect, held the entire process hostage by insisting that any policy solution be based on the private sector's capacity to make a profit on it — or, failing that, avoid any significant pain from it.

What might an alternative approach look like? For a start, it would entail a large-scale reversal of the trends of privatization, commodification, and marketization that have stood at the heart of neoliberal policy frameworks for the past generation, and a reclaiming of greater public ownership and democratic control over key economic sectors. In each of the major sectors implicated in the climate crisis (energy, transportation, agriculture, buildings, and industry), it would entail a much greater role for direct state intervention — whether federal, provincial, or municipal — both in terms of actively regulating and curtailing polluting industries, materials, and processes, and, in particular, directly funding new low-carbon infrastructures.

Doing all of this will require a fundamentally new framework for climate policy — one in which state planning (aimed at achieving environmental goals and community needs) replaces the neoliberal objective of trying to guarantee profits for private investors. Under such a framework, governments would be allowed to invest in the future of their people, and "returns on investment" would be understood in terms of a safer climate, better health, cleaner air and water, and stronger public services. Such a shift towards a public goods-centred policy framework would liberate climate policy from the neoliberal illusion that the private sector will eventually solve this issue on its own and allow Canadians to begin democratically planning a deliberate and effective path through this problem.

These sorts of ideas will undoubtedly be resisted in light of neoliberalism's continued ideological dominance in Canada. But the reality is that it's simply too late to hope that some piecemeal market-based incentives will suddenly prompt a free market (dominated by incumbent dirty industries) to rapidly unleash the "unprecedented changes" considered necessary by the UN's Intergovernmental Panel on Climate Change. The evidence would tend to suggest that we have reached a point in this crisis where markets increasingly have to be brought under the control of institutions and rational democratic planning. It means, in short, that neoliberalism must be dumped on the proverbial ash heap of history.

The problem with capitalism & the environment

But there is one further question that all climate and environmental activists need to seriously consider. And that is the question of whether this problem could ever truly be solved within a strictly capitalist framework. This remains one of the most important and polarizing questions in scholarly debates around the environment today, and it thus serves as fitting question on which to end the book.

If you are of the view that capitalism can (or should) be the dominant economic framework the leads humanity through the climate crisis, there is an entire body of scholarly literature (ecological modernization theory) that generally backs your point of view (see Chapter 5). According to advocates of this position, fossil fuels and GHG-intensive industries are merely an *incidental* aspect of modern capitalism, and it is easy enough to imagine a better form of capitalism that could make huge sums of profit from cleaner energy sources and industries. Advocates further note that, historically, capitalism has proved remarkably capable of accumulating through its own crises, and its profit motive and capacity for innovation *should* make it uniquely qualified to generate the rapid process of decarbonization that is required. Many advocates of a capitalist-led solution thus argue that the key task is merely to create a reformed version of capitalism in which better regulatory conditions and incentives are able to guide the system in this direction.

While this may be a tempting argument, it is worth acknowledging that capitalism would *only* solve its climate problem in order to ensure the continuity of ceaseless economic growth — which capitalism always requires in order to survive. Indeed, advocates of a capitalist-led solution to the crisis tend to resist this basic conclusion. But it is important for all environmentalists to appreciate that capitalism, as a system, can *never stop growing.* A capitalist system that fails to grow is one that enters into prolonged recession and crisis. It is one that sees corporate profitability decline, unemployment increase, tax revenues dry up, and states enter into fiscal crises in which they can no longer provide services or maintain their basic functions. In short, a capitalist system that fails to grow is a capitalist system that is dying.

So, obviously, clean growth is always preferable to dirty growth. But an equally vast and opposing body of scholarly literature within the anti-capitalist tradition provides a helpful reminder that the we simply cannot have unlimited growth within a finite planet (see, e.g., Foster 2006; O'Connor 1991; Schnaiberg 2000; Kovel 2006). Nature will never accommodate it, and while capitalism *may* someday prove capable of pressing pause on the climate problem (though, as noted above, this shows no signs of occurring), it will nevertheless continue to stumble heedlessly from one environmental crisis to another — species extinction, resource depletion, and perhaps eventually the full collapse of the biosphere. This arises not from the whim or malice of individual businesses or industries, but rather from capitalism's basic requirement to ceaselessly expand and promote endless mass production and consumption of unnecessary commodities. In short, it stems from capitalism's very DNA, and thus the capitalist system is the central obstacle in the transition to an ecologically sustainable economy.

This being the case, the only real solution to the environmental crisis is the creation of economies that are *not* dependent upon ceaseless growth, but rather oriented towards meeting the needs of communities, individuals, and the biosphere at large. All production and consumption in such a society would be undertaken as a *means* to achieving that goal, not simply as an *end* in itself — as is the case under capitalism. Contrary to capitalism's logic, the anti-capitalist tradition reminds us that human needs are not unlimited. And, as a result, it makes no sense to prop-up a system of production that is constantly trying to create fake needs for ephemeral consumer goods that will rapidly make their way to a landfill shortly after their purchase.

In this context, a low-carbon, sustainable and just economy requires not only cleaner technologies and methods of production, it also requires a completely new way of organizing our societies, understanding ourselves, and relating to each other and our fellow inhabitants of the biosphere. It requires reorienting our entire system of cultural values, and replacing them with ones not dependent upon ceaseless material growth. It requires a rigorous form of representative democracy with complete public control over production and planning. In short, it requires not only imagining but demanding other possible worlds.

CARBON TAX VS. CAP-AND-TRADE

One of the most commonly asked questions about contemporary climate policy is, what's the difference between a carbon tax and a cap-and-trade system? And, should environmentalists advocate for one over the other — or perhaps neither at all?

Both approaches emerge from a similar assumption in the writing of so-called market environmentalist thinkers. The assumption is that, if there is no monetary cost associated with emitting greenhouse gases, then businesses and households will just simply pollute at will, since they have no economic incentive to behave responsibly. The resolution, in their view, is simply to assign a price to polluting activities (either through a carbon tax or a cap-and-trade system), and thereby provide a financial incentive for polluters to change their behaviour.

While the two approaches derive from the same line of thinking, there are key differences between the two. With a carbon tax, the government simply sets a price on carbon emissions, and businesses (and sometimes households, depending on the scope of the policy) are forced to incur the penalties associated with burning carbon. If the price is high enough, it should incentivize them to reduce their emissions by, for example, investing in cleaner technologies or cutting down on unnecessary polluting.

By contrast, with a cap-and-trade system, the government sets a maximum level of carbon that can be emitted across the economy (a cap), then distributes "emissions permits" among polluting firms. Firms must have a permit to cover each unit of carbon they emit, which can be obtained either through an initial allocation from the government (*sometimes* via auction), or through trading with other firms who are looking to sell their excess permits. According to the logic, some firms will find it cheaper to simply reduce their emissions, and they can sell their extra permits to firms who find it cheaper just to buy more permits. While the "cap" is set by the government in advance, the "price" of the permits typically fluctuates according to supply and demand for the limited permits.

A common (and fairly obvious) follow-up question tends to be, which of the two is more effective? The answer is that it depends. Carbon taxes have the advantage of being considerably easier to design and implement — as governments can simply impose the tax and use existing administrative structures to collect and enforce it — and are much easier for both individuals and businesses to understand. As a result, advocates of a carbon tax insist it is superior because it is more transparent, guarantees that a minimum price will always be charged for emitting carbon, requires minimal government bureaucracy to oversee it, and is not subject to the vagaries of fluctuating permit prices.

Those advocating cap-and-trade note that, while carbon taxes provide certainty about the *price* being charged, there is no guarantee about the amount of actual emissions reductions. They note that cap-and-trade is superior because, by setting an overall cap, the government can directly set limits on the amount of carbon pollution that will be emitted. Moreover, because there is so much potential profit to be made in the design and execution of these markets (for example, financial firms can make commissions on trades, selling futures, etc., while regulated firms can make money selling excess permits), cap-and-trade is much more politically viable than a tax.

The experiences of the two approaches around the world nicely demonstrate the relative vices and virtues of each. Cap-and-trade programs have indeed been easier to establish in light of the powerful political coalitions they are able to forge. Yet, predictably, they are considerably more vulnerable to serious design flaws given the enormous amounts of industry lobbying that goes on around their creation. For instance, large cap-and-trade systems like the European Union Emissions Trading Scheme or the Regional Greenhouse Gas Initiative in the Northeastern US have been saddled with weak caps and overly generous allocations of permits to regulated entities (because, indeed, industries insisted upon this). As a result, permit prices have remained far too low to generate any serious reductions in carbon pollution. Carbon taxes, by contrast, have been much more difficult to implement and sustain (because, as we've seen in Canada, they are easily attacked by right-wing politicians as an onerous tax on hard working families), and where they have been implemented, the price has often remained far too low to incentivize better behaviour.

So, which approach is better? The simple answer is that it really depends on how each is designed. For example, what is the carbon price set at? What sectors are forced to incur the carbon price and which are exempt? How are the revenues being used? Are they being invested in clean energy infrastructure or given away in the form of tax breaks? In the case of cap-and-trade, it is crucial to ask if the system is littered with loopholes designed to make the scheme basically worthless. If both approaches are designed properly, they *can be* equally helpful in reducing emissions. But, by the same token, if both are designed poorly, they will be equally unhelpful. While good examples of both do exist, the overall global experience has been poor. According to the World Bank, as of 2017, in three-quarters of cases where carbon prices existed, they were no more than $10 per tonne, which is far too low to incentivize any meaningful change (World Bank 2017). While carbon prices can be a small and potentially helpful part of a much broader climate policy, there is little reason to believe that they can be the only (or even the central) feature (see Chapter 6).

REFERENCES

Abacus Data. 2015. "What Keeps Us Awake at Night: Top National Issues." <http://abacusdata.ca/what-keeps-us-awake-top-national-issues/>.

Angus Reid. 2016. "Battle of the Ballots: Two Alternate Voting Systems Seen as Competitive to First Past the Post." <http://angusreid.org/electoral-reform/>.

Bakvis, Herman, and Douglas Brown. 2010. "Policy Coordination in Federal Systems: Comparing Intergovernmental Processes and Outcomes in Canada and the United States." *Publius: Journal of Federalism*, 40, 3: 484–507.

Barnes, Andre. 2011. Youth Voter Turnout in Canada: Trends and Issues. Library of Parliament. <http://www.parl.gc.ca/Content/LOP/ResearchPublications/2010-19-e.htm>.

Bélanger, Alexis. 2011. "Canadian Federalism in the Context of Climate Change." *Constitutional Forum*, 20, 1: 21–31.

Black, David, and Greg Donaghy. 2010. "Manifestations of Canadian Mutilateralism." *Foreign Policy,* Spring: 1–8.

Blair, David. 2016. "The Framing of International Competitiveness in Canada's Climate Change Policy: Trade-Off or Synergy?" *Climate Policy*, 17, 6: 764–780.

Borger, Julian. 2001. "Bush Kills Global Warming Treaty." *The Guardian*, March 29. <https://www.theguardian.com/environment/2001/mar/29/globalwarming.usnews>.

___. 2015. "Climate Change Policy in Manitoba: A Small Province Looking to 'Punch above its Weight." *Manitoba Law Journal,* 38, 2: 155–183.

Boyd, David. 2002. "Stop the Dirty Dancing." *Globe and Mail*, May 24. <https://beta.theglobeandmail.com/opinion/stop-the-dirty-dancing/article754847/?ref=http://www.theglobeandmail.com&>.

Braungart, Michael, and William McDonough. 2002. *Cradle to Cradle. Remaking the Way We Make Things*. New York: North Point Press.

Broadhead, Lee-Anne. 2011. "Canada as a Rogue State: Its Shameful Performance on Climate Change." *International Journal*, 56, 3: 461–480.

Brown, Douglas. 2012. "Cooperative versus Competitive Federalism: Outcomes and Consequences of Intergovernmental Relations on Climate Change Issues in Canada." *Zeitschrift für Kanada-Studien*, 32, 2: 9–27. <http://www.kanada-studien.org/wp-content/uploads/2012/12/01_Brown.pdf>.

Brown, Douglas. 2012. "Comparative Climate Change Policy and Federalism: An

Overview." *Review of Policy Research*, 29, 3: 322–333.

Bulkeley, H., and M. Betsill. 2003. *Cities and Climate Change: Urban Sustainability and Global Environmental Governance*. London: Routledge.

Burck, Jan, Franziska Martin, Christoph Bals, and Niklas Hohne. 2018. "Climate Change Performance Index." Climate Action Network.

Cameron, David, and Richard Simeon. 2002. "Intergovernmental Relations in Canada: The Emergence of Collaborative Federalism." *Publius: The Journal of Federalism*, 32, 2: 49–72.

Canadian Press. 2017. "Focus Groups Confused, Contradictory over Marquee Liberal Carbon Pricing Policy." *Calgary Herald*, January 11. <https://calgaryherald.com/business/local-business/focus-groups-confused-contradictory-over-marquee-liberal-carbon-pricing-policy>.

Cardinal, Jesse. 2014. "The Tar Sands Healing Walk." In Stephen D'Arcy, Toban Black, Tony Weiss, and Joshua Kahn Russell (eds.), *A Line in the Tar Sands: Struggles for Environmental Justice*. Toronto: Between the Lines Press.

Carter, Angela. 2007. "Cursed by Oil? Institutions and Environmental Impacts in Alberta's Tar Sands." <https://www.cpsa-acsp.ca/papers-2007/Carter.pdf>.

Chalifour, Nathalie. 2008. "Making Federalism Work for Climate Change: Canada's Division of Powers over Carbon Taxes." *National Journal of Constitutional Law*, 22: 119.

Chaloux, Annie. 2015. "Canada's Multiple Voices Diplomacy in Climate Change Negotiations: A Focus on Québec." *International Negotiation*, 2: 291–318.

Christoff, Peter, and Robyn Eckersley. 2011. "Comparing State Responses." In John Dryzek, David Scholsberg, and Richard Norgaard (eds.), *The Oxford Handbook of Climate Change and* Society. Oxford: Oxford University Press.

Clapp, Jennier and Peter Dauvergne. 2005. *Paths to a Green World: The Political Economy of the Global Environment*. Cambridge: MIT Press.

Climate Action Tracker. 2019. Canada. <https://climateactiontracker.org/countries/canada/>.

Conference Board of Canada. 2016. "How Canada Performs: Innovation." <http://www.conferenceboard.ca/hcp/details/innovation.aspx>.

___. 2017. "Canadian Greenhouse Gas Emissions." <https://www.conferenceboard.ca/hcp/Details/Environment/greenhouse-gas-emissions.aspx?AspxAutoDetectCookieSupport=1>.

Dabbs, Frank. 2006. "Ralph Klein's Real Legacy." *Alberta Views* (September).

Dodman, D., and D. Satterthwaite. 2009. "Climate Change: Are Cities Really to Blame?" *Urban World*, 1: 12–13.

Ekos Research. 2016. "Canadian Attitudes toward Energy and Pipelines."

Environics Institute. 2016. "Canadian Public Opinion on Governance 2016." <http://www.environicsinstitute.org/uploads/institute-projects/canadian%20public%20opinion%20on%20governance%202016%20-%20final%20report%20-%20june%2017-2016.pdf>.

Environment and Climate Change Canada. 2017. "Canadian Environmental Sustainability Indicators. Greenhouse Gas Emissions." <https://www.ec.gc.ca/indicateurs-indicators/18F3BB9C-43A1-491E-9835-76C8DB9DDFA3/

GHGEmissions_EN.pdf>.

Esping-Andersen, Gøsta. 1990. *Three Worlds of Welfare Capitalism.* Princeton: Princeton University Press.

Fickling, Meera, and Jeffrey J. Schott. 2011. *nafta and Climate Change.* Peterson Institute for International Economics.

Ford, James, Tristan Pearce, Frank Duerden, Chris Furgal, and Barry Smith. 2010. "Climate Change Policy and Canada's Inuit Population: The Importance of and Opportunities for Adaptation." *Global Environmental Change,* 20: 171–191.

Foster, John Bellamy. 2006. "Marxism and Ecology." <https://monthlyreview.org/2015/12/01/marxism-and-ecology/>.

Frank, Thomas. 2004. *What's the Matter with Kansas? How Conservatives Won the Heart of America.* New York: Metropolitan Books.

Glicksman, Robert. 2010. "Anatomy of Industry Resistance to Climate Change: A Familiar Litany." *Global Environmental Change,* 20, 1: 177–191.

Goldwag, Arthur. 2012. *A History of Fear and Loathing on the Populist Right.* Chicago: Pantheon.

Gordon, David. 2015a. "An Uneasy Equilibrium: The Coordination of Climate Governance in Federated Systems." *Global Environmental Politics,* 15, 2 (May): 121–141.

____. 2015b. "Lament for a Network? Cities and Networked Climate Governance in Canada." *Environment and Planning C: Government and Policy,* 30: 571–590.

Gordon, David, and Douglas Macdonald. 2011. "Institutions and Federal Climate Change Governance: A Comparison of the Intergovernmental Coordination of Australia and Canada." Paper presented at the annual meeting of the Canadian Political Science Association, University of Waterloo, 18 May 2011. <https://www.cpsa-acsp.ca/papers-2011/Gordon-Macdonald.pdf>.

Gordon, Todd. 2007. *Cops, Crime and Capitalism.* Halifax: Fernwood Publishing.

____. 2010. *Imperialist Canada.* Toronto: arp Books.

Gordon, Todd, and Jeffrey R. Webber. 2016. *Blood of Extraction: Canadian Imperialism in Latin America.* Halifax: Fernwood Publishing.

Gore, Christopher. 2010. "The Limits and Opportunities of Networks: Municipalities and Canadian Climate Change Policy." *Review of Policy Research,* 27, 1: 27–46.

Government of Canada. 2002. "A Climate Change Plan for Canada." <http://manitobawildlands.org/pdfs/CCPlanforCAN27Nov02.pdf>.

____. 2013. "Union Coverage in Canada, 2012." <http://tinyurl.com/j9nb2lg>.

____. 2016a. "Canada's Merchandise Trade with the World." Library of Parliament Research.

____. 2016b. "Environment Canada Briefing Book." <https://www.canada.ca/en/environment-climate-change/corporate/briefing.html>.

____. 2017. "Canadian Environmental Protection Act of 1999." <http://www.ec.gc.ca/lcpe-cepa/default.asp?lang=En&n=26a03bfa-1>.

Greenblatt, Alan. 2016. "In Life after Coal, Appalachia Attempts to Reinvent Itself." December. <http://www.governing.com/topics/finance/gov-coal-trump-appalachia-economy.html>.

Guber, D. 2003. *The Grassroots of a Green Revolution: Polling America on the Environment.* Cambridge: MIT Press.

Haley, B. 2011. "From Staples Trap to Carbon Trap: Canada's Peculiar Form of Carbon Lock-In." *Studies in Political Economy,* 88: 97–132.

Hall, Peter. 1997. "The Role of Interests, Institutions and Ideas in the Comparative Political Economy of the Industrialized Nations." In M.I. Lichbach and A.S. Zuckerman (eds.), *Comparative Politics: Rationality, Culture and Structure.* Cambridge: Cambridge University Press.

Hall, Peter, and David Soskice (eds.). 2001. *Varieties of Capitalism: The Institutional Foundations of Comparative Advantage.* Oxford: Oxford University Press.

Harrison, Kathryn. 2002. *Passing the Buck: Federalism and Canadian Environmental Policy.* Vancouver: UBC Press.

___. 2006. "The Struggle between Ideas and Self-Interest: Canada's Ratification and Implementation of the Kyoto Protocol." Annual Meeting of the International Studies Association, San Diego, California, March 22–26, 2006.

___. 2007. "The Road Not Taken: Climate Change Policy in Canada and the United States." *Global Environmental Politics,* 7, 4: 92–117.

___. 2010. "The Struggle of Ideas and Self-Interest in Canadian Climate Policy." In Kathryn Harrison and Lisa McIntosh Sundstrom (eds.), *Global Commons, Domestic Decisions.* MIT Press.

___. 2012a. "A Tale of Two Taxes: The Fate of Environmental Tax Reform in Canada." *Review of Policy Research,* 29, 3: 383–407.

___. 2012b. "Multilevel Governance and American Influence on Canadian Climate Policy: The California Effect vs. the Washington Effect." *Zeitschrift fur Kanada-Studien,* 32, 2: 45–64.

___. 2013. "Federalism and Climate Policy Innovation: A Critical Assessment." *Canadian Public Policy,* 39: 95–108.

Harrison, Kathryn, and Lisa McIntosh Sundstrom. 2007. "The Comparative Politics of Climate Change." *Global Environmental Politics,* 7, 4: 1–18.

Harrison, Peter. 2009. "Median Wages in Canada and the US. Centre for Study of Living Standards." <http://www.csls.ca/notes/note2009-2.pdf>.

Harvey, David. 2007. *A Brief History of Neoliberalism.* Oxford: Oxford University Press.

Hayter, R., and T. Barnes. 2001. "Canada's Resource Economy." *Canadian Geographer,* 45, 1: 36–41.

Houle, David, Erick Lachapelle, and Mark Purdon. 2015. "The Comparative Politics of Sub-Federal Cap-and-Trade: Implementing the Western Climate Initiative." *Global Environmental Politics,* 15, 3: 49–73.

Houle, David, Erick Lachapelle, and Barry Rabe. 2014. "Climate Compared: Sub-Federal Dominance on a Global Issue." In Martin Papillon, Jennifer Walner, and Stephen White (eds.), *Comparing Canada: Citizens, Government, and Policy.* Vancouver: UBC Press.

Houle, David, and Douglas Macdonald. 2011. "Comprendre le choix des instruments de politiques publiques en matière de changement climatique au Canada." *Télescope,* 17, 2: 183–208.

Huber, Joseph. 2004. *New Technologies and Environmental Innovation*. Cheltenham: Edward Elgar.

Innis, Harold. 1956. "The Teaching of Economic History in Canada." In M.Q. Innis (ed.), *Essays in Canadian Economic History*. University of Toronto Press.

IEA (International Energy Agency). 2016. "World Energy Investment 2016." <https://www.iea.org/newsroom/news/2016/september/world-energy-investment-2016.html>.

International Institute for Sustainable ⬛Development. 2016. "Unpacking Canada's Fossil Fuel Subsidies: Their Size, Impacts, and What Should Happen Next." <https://www.iisd.org/faq/unpacking-canadas-fossil-fuel-subsidies/>.

Ipsos Mori. 2015. "Global Trends 2014: Navigating the New." <https://www.ipsos.com/sites/default/files/publication/1970-01/ipsos-mori-global-trends-2014.pdf>.

Johnson, Tracy, and Kyle Bakx. 2016. "Canadians Conflicted about 3 Es: Environment, Energy and the Economy." CBC News, Mar 14.

Karp, Jeffrey, and Susan A. Banducci. 1999. "The Impact of Proportional Representation on Turnout: Evidence from New Zealand." *Australian Journal of Political Science*, 34, 3: 363–377.

Keating, Tom. 2002. *Canada and World Order: The Multilateralist Tradition in Canadian Foreign Policy*. Don Mills: Oxford University Press.

___. 2003. *Multilateralism and Canadian Foreign Policy: A Reassessment*. Canadian Defense and Foreign Affairs Institute.

Kern, K., and H. Bulkeley. 2009. "Cities, Europeanization and Multi-Level Governance: Governing Climate Change Through Transnational Municipal Networks." *Journal of Common Market Studies*, 47: 309–332.

Kirchhoff, Denis, and Leonard J.S. Tsuji. 2014. "Reading Between the Lines of the 'Responsible Resource Development' Rhetoric: The Use of Omnibus Bills to 'Streamline' Canadian Environmental Legislation." *Impact Assessment and Project Appraisal*, 32, 2: 108–120.

Kovel, Joel. 2006. *The Enemy of Nature: The End of Capitalism or the End of the World*. <http://www.greanvillepost.com/special/Kovel,%20Enemy%20of%20Nature%20(2007).pdf>.

Laboucan-Massimo, Melina. 2014. "Awaiting Justice: The Ceaseless Struggle of the Lubicon Cree." In Stephen D'Arcy, Toban Black, Tony Weiss, and Joshua Kahn Russell (eds.), *A Line in the Tar Sands: Struggles for Environmental Justice*. Toronto: Between the Lines Press.

Lachapelle, Erick, Christopher Borick, and Barry Rabe. 2013. "Public Attitudes toward Climate Science and Climate Policy in Federal Systems: Canada and the United States Compared." *Review of Policy Research*, 29 3: 335–358.

___. 2014. "2013 Canada–US Comparative Climate Opinion Survey." Canada 2020. <http://canada2020.ca/wp-content/uploads/2014/03/Canada-2020-Background-Paper-Climate-Poll-Key-Findings-March-3-2014.pdf>.

Lachapelle, Erick, Robert MacNeil, and Matthew Paterson. 2017. "The Political Economy of Decarbonisation: From Green Energy 'Race' to Green 'Division of Labour'. *New Political Economy*, 22, 3: 311–327.

Lameman, Crystal. 2014. "Kihci Pikiskwewin — Speaking the Truth." In Stephen

D'Arcy, Toban Black, Tony Weiss, and Joshua Kahn Russell (eds.), *A Line in the Tar Sands: Struggles for Environmental Justice*. Toronto: Between the Lines Press. <https://www.cfr.org/content/publications/attachments/Oil_Sands_CSR47.pdf>.

Lowrey, Annie. 2014. "What's the Matter with Eastern Kentucky?" *New York Times*, June 26. <https://www.nytimes.com/2014/06/29/magazine/whats-the-matter-with-eastern-kentucky.html>.

Macdonald, Douglas. 2001. "The Business Campaign to Prevent Kyoto Ratification." Paper presented at the annual meeting of the Canadian Political Science Association, Dalhousie University, May 31, 2001.

____. 2008. "Explaining the Failure of Canadian Climate Policy." In H. Compston and I. Bailey (eds.), *Turning Down the Heat: The Politics of Climate Policy in Affluent Democracies*. New York: Palgrave.

____. 2009. "The Government of Canada's Search for Environmental Legitimacy: 1971–2008." *International Journal of Canadian Studies*, 39/40: 191–210.

____. 2015a. "Ontario Renewable Energy and Climate Change Policy in the Canadian Intergovernmental and North American Contexts." Paper prepared for the Climate Change and Renewable Energy Policy in the EU and Canada Workshop held at Carleton University, Ottawa on October 1–2, 2015.

____. 2015b. "The Challenge of Canadian Climate and Energy Federalism: Explaining the Collapse of the Canadian National Climate Change Process, 1998–2002." Paper presented at the annual meeting of the Canadian Political Science Association, June 4, 2015.

MacNeil, Robert. 2014a. "The Decline of Canadian Environmental Regulation: Neoliberalism and the Staples Bias." *Studies in Political Economy*, 93 (Spring): 79–104.

____. 2014b. "Canadian Environmental Policy Under Conservative Majority Rule." *Environmental Politics*, 23, 1: 174–178.

____. 2016. "Death and Environmental Taxes: Why Market Environmentalism Fails in Liberal Market Economies." *Global Environmental Politics*, 16, 1: 21–37.

MacNeil, Robert, and Matthew Paterson. 2016. "This Changes Everything? Canadian Climate Policy and the 2015 Election." *Environmental Politics*, 25, 3: 553–557.

____. 2018. "Trudeau's Canada and the Challenge of Decarbonisation." *Environmental Politics*, 25, 3: 553–557.

McCarthy, Shawn. 2017. "Two-Thirds of Canadians Approve of Ottawa's Climate Regulations." *Globe and Mail* April 10. <https://www.theglobeandmail.com/news/politics/two-thirds-of-canadians-approve-of-ottawas-climate-regulations-poll/article34205335/>.

McCreary, Tyler. 2014. "Beyond Token Recognition: The Growing Movement against the Northern Gateway Project." In Stephen D'Arcy, Toban Black, Tony Weiss, and Joshua Kahn Russell (eds.), *A Line in the Tar Sands: Struggles for Environmental Justice*. Toronto: Between the Lines Press.

Mildenberger, Matto, Peter Howe, Erik Lachapelle, Leah Stokes, et al. 2016. "The Distribution of Climate Change Public Opinion in Canada." ENVS Faculty Publications, Paper 1450.

Milner, Henry. 2009. "Does Proportional Representation Boost Turnout? A Political

Knowledge-based Explanation." Working paper presented at the Comparative Study of Electoral Systems (CSES) conference, University of Toronto, September 6, 2009.

Mol, Arthur. 2001, *Globalization and Environmental Reform: The Ecological Modernization of the Global Economy*, Cambridge: MIT Press.

Munroe, Kaija. 2010. *Business, Risk, and Carbon Pricing: Business Preference for Climate Change Instruments in Canada*. Sustainable Prosperity Background Report. <http://institute.smartprosperity.ca/sites/default/files/business-risk-and-carbon-pricing.pdf>.

___. 2016. *Business in A Changing Climate: Explaining Industry Support for Carbon Pricing*. Toronto: University of Toronto Press.

National Energy Board. 2012. "Energy Trade—Energy Facts." Government of Canada. <https://www.neb-one.gc.ca/bts/whwr/nbfctsht-eng.html>.

___. 2017. "Provincial and Territorial Energy Profiles." <https://www.neb-one.gc.ca/nrg/ntgrtd/mrkt/nrgsstmprfls/cda-eng.html>.

Natural Resources Canada. 2012. "Canada's Potash Industry." Government of Canada. <http://www.nrcan.gc.ca/media-room/news-release/2012/6427>.

Norris, Pippa. 1997. "Choosing Electoral Systems: Proportional, Majoritarian and Mixed Systems." *International Political Science Review*, 18, 3: 297–312.

North, Douglas. 1991. "Institutions." *Journal of Economic Perspectives,* 5, 1 (Winter): 97–112.

O'Connor, James. 1971. *The Fiscal Crisis of the State*. New York: Transaction Publishers.

___. 1991. "On the Two Contradictions of Capitalism." *Capitalism Nature Socialism,* 2, 3.

OECD. 2015. "Indicators of Employment Protection." <http://tinyurl.com/qyv4kw6>.

Paris, Roland. 2014. "Are Canadians Still Liberal Internationalists: Foreign Policy and Public Opinion in the Harper Era." *International Journal*, 69, 3: 274–307.

Paterson, Matthew. 2009. "Post Hegemonic Climate Politics." *British Journal of International Relations,* 11, 1: 140–158.

___. 2012. "Who and What Are Carbon Markets For? Politics and the Development of Climate Policy." *Climate Policy,* 12, 1: 82–97.

Peck, Jamie. 2001. "Neoliberalizing States: Thin Policies/Hard Outcomes." *Progress in Human Geography,* 25, 3: 445–455.

___. 2013. *Constructions of Neoliberal Reason*. Oxford: Oxford University Press.

PIPSC (Professional Institute of the Public Service of Canada). 2011. "Harper Government Cuts to Science Overwhelmingly Detrimental and Out of Sync with Public's Priorities." <http://www.pipsc.ca/portal/page/portal/website/issues/science/vanishingscience>.

Purdon, Mark. 2015. "Advancing Comparative Climate Change Policy: Theory and Method." *Global Environmental Politics*, 15, 3: 1–26.

Rivers, Nic. 2009. "Impacts of Climate Policy on the Competitiveness of Canadian Industry: How Big and How to Mitigate?" *Energy Economics*, 32: 1092–1104.

Ross, Marc Howard. 2009. "Culture." In Mark Irving and Alan Zuckerman (eds.), *Comparative Political Analysis*, second edition. New York: Cambridge University

Press.

Saad-Filho, Alfredo, and Deborah Johnston (eds.). 2005. *Neoliberalism: A Critical Reader*. London: Pluto Press.

Schnaiberg, Allan. 2000. "The Treadmill of Production and the Environmental State." <http://www.ipr.northwestern.edu/publications/papers/urban-policy-and-community-development/docs/schnaiberg/treadmill-of-production.pdf>.

___. 2008a. "Canada and Kyoto: Independence or Indifference?" In Brian Bow and Patrick Lennox (eds.), *An Independent Foreign Policy for Canada? Challenges and Choices for the Future*. Toronto: University of Toronto Press.

___. 2008b. "Political Parties and Canadian Climate Change Policy." *International Journal*, Winter: 47–66.

Smith, Heather, and Douglas Macdonald. 2000. "Promises Made, Promises Broken: Questioning Canada's Commitments to Climate Change." *International Journal*, 55, 1: 107–124.

Spash, Clive. 2010. "The Brave New World of Carbon Trading." *New Political Economy*, 15, 2: 169–195.

Stanford, Jim. 2008. "Staples, Deindustrialization, and Foreign Investment: Canada's Economic Journey Back to the Future." *Studies in Political Economy*, 82: 7–34.

___. 2012. "A Cure for Dutch Disease: Active Sector Strategies for Canada's Economy, Alternative Federal Budget Technical Paper." Canadian Centre for Policy Alternatives.

Sweeny, Sean, and John Treat. 2019. "When Green Doesn't Grow: Facing up to the Failures of Profit-Driven Climate Policy." Centre for Research on Globalization. <https://www.globalresearch.ca/when-green-doesnt-grow-facing-up-to-the-failures-of-profit-driven-climate-policy/5664393>.

Taylor, Gray, and Michael Barrett. 2009. "Canada's Experience in Emissions Trading and Related Legal Issues." In David Freestone and Charlotte Streck (eds.), *Legal Aspects of Carbon Trading: Kyoto, Copenhagen and Beyond*. Oxford: Oxford University Press.

Vogel, David. 1995. *Trading Up: Consumer and Environmental Regulation in a Global Economy*. Harvard University Press.

Walsh, Bryan. 2011. "Bienveneu au Canada: Welcome to Your Friendly Neighborhood Petro-state." *Time Magazine*. <http://science.time.com/2011/12/14/bienvenue-au-canada-welcome-to-your-friendly-neighborhood-petrostate/>.

Way, Laura. 2011. "An Energy Superpower or a Super Sales Pitch? Building the Case Through an Examination of Canadian Newspaper Coverage of Oil Sands." *Canadian Political Science Review*, 5, 1: 74–98.

Wikimedia Commons. 2019. "First-past-the-post voting. <https://en.wikipedia.org/wiki/First-past-the post_voting#/media/File:Countries_That_Use_a_First_Past_the_Post_Voting_System.png>

World Bank. 2017. "Carbon Pricing Watch 2017." <https://openknowledge.worldbank.org/handle/10986/26565>.

Woynillowicz, D., and N. Lemphers. 2012. "In the Shadow of the Boom: How Oil Sands Development Is Reshaping Canada's Economy." *Pembina Institute*. <http://www.pembina.org /pub/2345>.

WTEX. 2018. "Canada's Top Ten Exports." <http://www.worldstopexports.com/canadas-top-exports/>.

Young, Nathan, and Aline Coutinho. 2013. "Government, Anti-Reflexivity, and the Construction of Public Ignorance about Climate Change: Australia and Canada Climate Change: Australia and Canada Compared." *Global Environmental Politics*, 13, 2: 89–108.

Young, Stephen. 2000. *The Emergence of Ecological Modernisation: Integrating the Environment and the Economy.* London: Routledge.

INDEX